Chile
& Easter Island

a Lonely Planet travel atlas

Chile & Easter Island – travel atlas

1st edition

Published by
Lonely Planet Publications
Head Office: PO Box 617, Hawthorn, Vic 3122, Australia
Branches: 155 Filbert St, Suite 251, Oakland, CA 94607, USA
             10 Barley Mow Passage, Chiswick, London W4 4PH, UK
             71 bis rue du Cardinal Lemoine, 75005 Paris, France

Cartography
Steinhart Katzir Publishers Ltd
Fax: 972-3-699-7562
email: 100264.721@compuserve.com

Printed by
Colorcraft Ltd, Hong Kong
Printed in China

Photographs
Wayne Bernhardson, Helen Hughes

Front Cover: Cerro Guane Guane, Parque Nacional Lauca (Wayne Bernhardson)
Back Cover: Lago Chungará & Volcán Parinacota, Parque Nacional Lauca (Wayne Bernhardson)
Title page: Cuernos del Paine, Parque Nacional Torres del Paine (Wayne Bernhardson)
Contents page: Sculpture, Antofagasta (Wayne Bernhardson)

First Published
January 1997

Although the authors and publisher have tried to make the information as accurate as possible, they accept no responsibility for any loss, injury or inconvenience sustained by any person using this book.

National Library of Australia Cataloguing in Publication Data

Bernhardson, Wayne.
    Chile & Easter Island travel atlas.

    1st ed.
    Includes index.
    ISBN 0 86442 517 1

    1. Chile - Maps, Tourist. 2. Chile - Road maps.
    3. Easter Island - Road maps. 4. Easter Island - Maps, Tourist.
    I. Title. (Series : Lonely Planet travel atlas).

912.83

Contents

Acknowledgements...4

Locator Maps..5-7
Map Legend...8-9
Maps..10-55

Getting Around Chile & Easter Island.................................56-57
Comment Circuler au Chili et à l'Île de Pâques....................58-59
Reisen in Chile und auf der Oster Insel..............................60-61
Cómo Movilizarse dentro de Chile e Isla de Pascua.............62-63
チリとイースター島の旅 64-65

Index..66-88

Wayne Bernhardson

Wayne Bernhardson was born in Fargo, North Dakota, grew up in Tacoma, Washington, and earned a PhD in geography at the University of California, Berkeley. He has travelled extensively in Mexico and Central and South America, and lived for extended periods in Chile, Argentina and the Falkland (Malvinas) Islands. His other LP credits include the *Chile & Easter Island* (3rd ed.), *Argentina, Uruguay & Paraguay* (2nd ed.), *Baja California* (3rd ed.) and *The Rocky Mountain States* (1st ed.) travel survival kits, and the 5th edition of *South America on a Shoestring*. Wayne resides in Oakland, California, with his affectionate Alaskan malamute, Gardel.

About this Atlas

This book is another addition to the Lonely Planet travel atlas series. Designed to tie in with the equivalent Lonely Planet guidebook, we hope that the *Chile & Easter Island travel atlas* helps travellers enjoy their trip even more. As well as detailed, accurate maps, this atlas also contains a multilingual map legend, useful travel information in five languages and a comprehensive index to ensure easy location-finding.

The maps were checked on the road by Wayne Bernhardson as part of his preparation for a new edition of Lonely Planet's *Chile & Easter Island – travel survival kit*.

From the Publishers

Thanks to Danny Schapiro, chief cartographer at Steinhart Katzir Publishers, who supervised production of this atlas. Liora Aharoni was responsible for the cartography. Iris Sardes prepared the index. At Lonely Planet, editorial checking of the maps and index was completed by Lou Byrnes. Sally Jacka was responsible for the cartographic checking. Louise Keppie-Klep completed the design, layout and cover design. The back cover map was drawn by Paul Clifton. Paul Smitz edited the getting around section and updated the index.

Lou Byrnes coordinated the translations. Thanks to translators Yoshiharu Abe, Christa Bouga-Hochstöger, Adrienne Costanzo, Pedro Diaz, Brad Felstead, Megan Fraser, Patricia Matthieu, Sergio Mariscal, Isabelle Muller, Penelope Richardson, and Karin Riederer.

Request

This atlas is designed to be clear, comprehensive and reliable. We hope you'll find it a worthy addition to your Lonely Planet travel library. Even if you don't, please let us know! We'd appreciate any suggestions you may have to make this product even better. Please complete and send us the feedback page at the back of this atlas to let us know exactly what you think.

Mapuche women in traditional dress from the Malalcahuelle community, between Temuco and Nueva Imperial

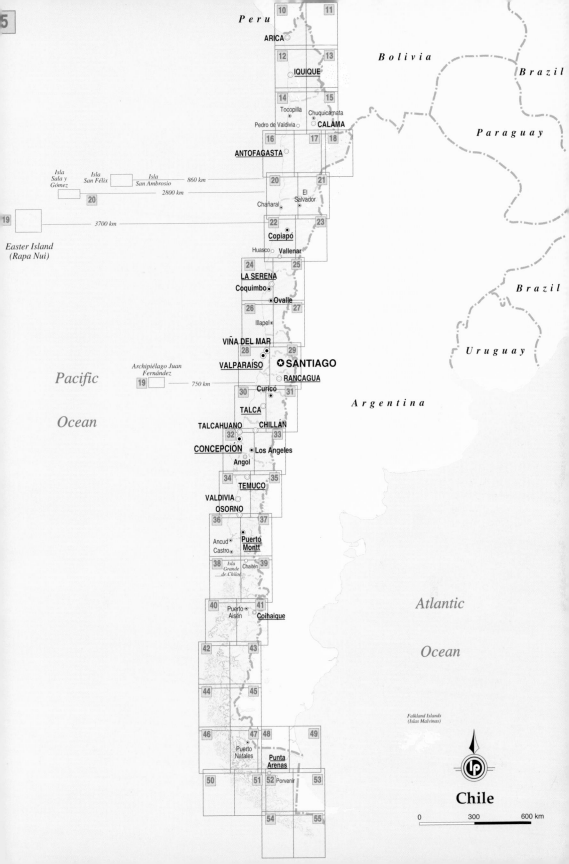

Peru

10
11

ARICA

Bolivia

Brazil

12
13

IQUIQUE

14
15

Tocopilla
Chuquicamata
Pedro de Valdivia
CALAMA

Paraguay

16
17
18

ANTOFAGASTA

Isla
Sala y
Gómez

Isla
San Félix

Isla
San Ambrosio   860 km

20
21

2800 km

20

El
Salvador

Chañaral

19   3700 km

22
23

Copiapó

**Easter Island
(Rapa Nui)**

Huasco   Vallenar

24
25

LA SERENA

Coquimbo
Ovalle

Brazil

26
27

Illapel

Pacific

VIÑA DEL MAR

28
29

Ocean

Archipiélago Juan
Fernández

VALPARAÍSO   ✪ **SANTIAGO**

Uruguay

19   750 km

RANCAGUA

30
31

Curicó

Argentina

TALCA

TALCAHUANO   **CHILLAN**

32
33

CONCEPCIÓN   Los Angeles

Angol

34
35

TEMUCO

VALDIVIA

OSORNO

36
37

Ancud
Castro
**Puerto
Montt**

38
39

Isla
Grande
de Chiloé   Chaitén

Atlantic

40
41

Puerto
Aisén   **Coihaique**

Ocean

42
43

44
45

Falkland Islands
(Islas Malvinas)

46
47
48
49

Puerto
Natales
**Punta
Arenas**   Porvenir

50
51
52
53

Chile

0   300   600 km

54
55

6

Peru

Bolivia

Argentina

Pacific

Ocean

Tropic of Capricorn

76°W 74°W 72°W 70°W 68°W 66°W 64°W

20°S

22°S

24°S

26°S

28°S

30°S

32°S

36°S

ARICA

Parque Nacional Lauca

Reserva Nacional Las Vicuñas

Monumento Natural Salar de Surire

Tarapacá

Reserva Nacional Pampa del Tamarugal

Parque Nacional Isluga

Salar de Uyuni

IQUIQUE

Salar de Pintados

Reserva Nacional Pampa del Tamarugal

Ollague

Tocopilla

María Elena

Chuquicamata

CALAMA

Pedro de Valdivia

San Pedro de Atacama

Mejillones

Baquedano

ANTOFAGASTA

Salar de Atacama

Antofagasta

Parque Nacional Pan de Azúcar

El Salvador

Chañaral

Huasco

Copiapó

Atacama

Vallenar

Parque Nacional Rapa Nui

Easter Island (Rapa Nui)

LA SERENA

Coquimbo

Vicuña

Parque Nacional Fray Jorge

Ovalle

Combarbalá

Coquimbo

Illapel

Valparaíso

La Ligua

La Calera

San Felipe

VIÑA DEL MAR

Los Andes

VALPARAÍSO

Parque Nacional La Campana

Reserva Nacional Laguna Peñuelas

SANTIAGO

San Antonio

MAIPÚ

PUENTE ALTO

Reserva Nacional Río Clarillo

Melipilla

SAN BERNARDO

Santiago

Archipiélago Juan Fernández

Parque Nacional Juan Fernández

O'Higgins

Embalse Rapel

Pichilemu

Rengo

RANCAGUA

Reserva Nacional Río Los Cipreses

San Fernando

Chimbarongo

Curicó

Molina

Maule

Área de Protección Radal Siete Tazas

Parque Gil de Vilches

Constitución

TALCA

Monumento Natural

San Javier

San Clemente

Reserva Nacional Federico Albert

Reserva Nacional Los Ruiles

Linares

Laguna del Maule

Biobío

Cauquenes

Parral

Coelemu

Tomé

TALCAHUANO

CONCEPCIÓN

Penco

CHILLÁN

Coronel

Chiguayante

	Major Highway
	Highway
	Regional Road
	Railway

Northern Chile

0   150   300 km

MAP LEGEND

Number of Inhabitants:

SANTIAGO		>500,000
VIÑA DEL MAR	◉	250,000 - 500,000
TEMUCO	◎	100,000 - 250,000
Puerto Montt	◉	50,000 - 100,000
Los Andes	◎	25,000 - 50,000
Villarrica	◉	10,000 - 25,000
Vicuña	○	5,000 - 10,000
San Pedro de Atacama	○	< 5,000

SANTIAGO
Capital City
Capitale
Hauptstadt
Capital
首都

★ Capital City (Locator map)
Capitale (Carte de situation)
Hauptstadt (Orientierungskarte)
Capital (Mapa de Situación)
首都（地図上の位置）

VALPARAÍSO
Regional Capital
Capitale de régionale
Regionalhauptstadt
Capital Regional
地方都市

Talagante
Provincial Capital
Capitale de Province
Landeshauptstadt
Capital Provincial
地方の中心地

International Boundary
Limites Internationales
Staatsgrenze
Límite Internacional
国境

Regional Boundary
Limite régionale
Gebietsgrenze
Límite Regional
地域の境界

Provincial Boundary
Limites de la Province
Landesgrenze
Límite Provincial
地方の境界

Ferry Route
Route de ferry
Fährroute
Transbordador
フェリーの航路

Motorway
Route Nationale
Femstraße
Autopista
高速幹線道路

Main Highway
Route Principale
Landstraße
Carretera Principal
主要な国道

Main Road
Route Régionale
Regionale Fernstraße
Camino Regional
主要道路

Secondary Road
Route Secondaire
Nebenstraße
Camino Secundario
二級道路

Passenger Railway
Train de passagers
Personenzug
Ferrocarril de pasajeros
乗客用鉄道

Freight Railway
Train de marchandises
Güterzug
Ferrocarril de mercancías
貨物用鉄道

Malvilla
Railway station
Gare Ferroviaire
Bahnhof
Estación de Ferrocarril
駅

Ch 45 71 RN 40 RP 80
Chile Argentina
Route Number
Numérotation Routière
Routennummer
Número de Ruta
道路の番号

40
Distance in Kilometres
Distance en Kilomètres
Entfernung in Kilometern
Distancia en Kilómetros
距離（km）

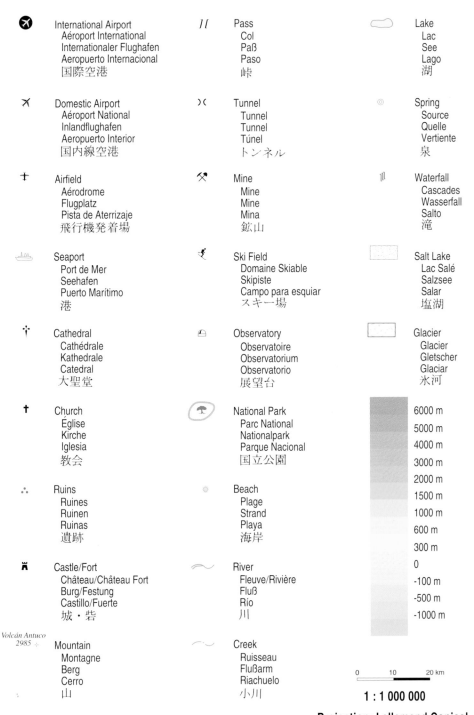

International Airport
Aéroport International
Internationaler Flughafen
Aeropuerto Internacional
国際空港

Domestic Airport
Aéroport National
Inlandflughafen
Aeropuerto Interior
国内線空港

Airfield
Aérodrome
Flugplatz
Pista de Aterrizaje
飛行機発着場

Seaport
Port de Mer
Seehafen
Puerto Marítimo
港

Cathedral
Cathédrale
Kathedrale
Catedral
大聖堂

Church
Église
Kirche
Iglesia
教会

Ruins
Ruines
Ruinen
Ruinas
遺跡

Castle/Fort
Château/Château Fort
Burg/Festung
Castillo/Fuerte
城・砦

Volcán Antuco
2985
Mountain
Montagne
Berg
Cerro
山

Pass
Col
Paß
Paso
峠

Tunnel
Tunnel
Tunnel
Túnel
トンネル

Mine
Mine
Mine
Mina
鉱山

Ski Field
Domaine Skiable
Skipiste
Campo para esquiar
スキー場

Observatory
Observatoire
Observatorium
Observatorio
展望台

National Park
Parc National
Nationalpark
Parque Nacional
国立公園

Beach
Plage
Strand
Playa
海岸

River
Fleuve/Rivière
Fluß
Río
川

Creek
Ruisseau
Flußarm
Riachuelo
小川

Lake
Lac
See
Lago
湖

Spring
Source
Quelle
Vertiente
泉

Waterfall
Cascades
Wasserfall
Salto
滝

Salt Lake
Lac Salé
Salzsee
Salar
塩湖

Glacier
Glacier
Gletscher
Glaciar
氷河

6000 m
5000 m
4000 m
3000 m
2000 m
1500 m
1000 m
600 m
300 m
0
-100 m
-500 m
-1000 m

0   10   20 km

1 : 1 000 000

Projection: Lallemand Conical

A   B   C   D

1

23°S

Caleta Gualaguala

Hornitos

Caleta Chacaya

Punta Angamos

▲14▲

Bahía de
Mejillones
del Sur

12

Quebrada de Mejillones

Elenita

70°W

Porvenir

Morro
Mejillones
766

Mejillones

Punta Lobería

18   24

Guanaquillo

Caleta Herradura
de Mejillones

Los
Placeres

Sierra Miranda

2

Caleta Bandurria
del Sur

Las
Cruces

Peninsula Mejillones

35

Mantos
Blancos

5

Punta Lagartos

Cerro
Moreno

Isla Santa María

✈

72

Latorre

Juan
López

Bahía
Moreno

Punta Tetas

Punta Jorge

Reserva
Nacional
La Chimba

Uribe

Sala
de
Navid

Monumento Natural
La Portada

26

O'Higgins

ANTOFAGASTA

3

Playa Huáscar

28

Caleta Coloso

Pampa
Arturo P

Punta Coloso

La Negra

Caleta Bolfín
Cabo Jara

Ensueño

53

Pacific

5

Antofagast

Ocean

4

24°S

Caleta Agua Dulce

Cerro Cristales
⊹ 2135

Cerro Tres Te
⊹ 2333

Caleta Agua Salada

Caleta El Cobre

Caleta El Cobre

55

Sierra Remiendos

Agua Bu

Caleta Blanco
Encalada

Blanco
Encalada

Cerro Ventarrones
2622 ⊹

Cerro Vicuña
Mackenna
⊹ 3114

5

Caleta Tragagente

Punta Botija

Caleta
Botija

Cerro La Chira
⊹ 2559

Punta Dos Reyes

1

Paranal

Cerro Paranal
2664 ⊹

58

125

Sierra Vicuña Mackenna

Caleta Colorada

6

Punta Plata

El
Médano

▼20▼

Reserva
Nacional
El Paposo

Sierra Amarilla

Punta Posallaves

Tor
2

Cabo
Norte

Caleta
Hanga Oteo

Punta
San Juan

Caleta
Anakena

Anakena

Bahía de
La Perouse

Maunga Terevaja
507

Ovahe

Ahu Tepeu

Maunga Pukatikei
370

Cabo O'Higgins

Volcán
Rano A-Roi

Cabo Cumming

Motu Tautara

**Península
Poike**

Cabo Roggewein

**Caverna de las Dos Ventanas
(Ana Ipu Maengo)**

Parque Nacional
Rapa Nui

Volcán
Rano Raraku

**Ahu
Tongariki**

29

Motu Marotiri

Puna
Pau

Maunga
Otu

Caleta
Hotuiti

Hanga Roa

Vaitea

Punta Roa

Maunga
Tuutapu

Punta Baquedano

20

Punta Baja

5

Hanga
Vinapu

Punta
Redonda

Orongo

Ahu Vinapu

Motu Kao
Kao

Rano Kau
410

Motu
Iti

Cabo
Sur

Easter Island

Motu
Nui

(Rapa Nui)

0   2.5   5   7.5 km

1 : 250 000

Archipiélago Juan Fernández

Bahía
La Vaquería

Punta Norte

Punta Salinas

Isla Robinson Crusoe

Cerro Alto
600

Bahía
Cumberland

Islote
Juanango

Cerro
Tres Puntas

San Juan
Bautista

Punta
Tunquillax

Cerro
Agudo

Punta
Hueso Ballena

Islote
Vinillo

Punta
Isla

Punta
Truenos

Bahía
Tierras
Blancas

Islote Los
Chamelos

Islote El
Verdugo

Punta
O'Higgins

Ensenada
Toltén

Cabo Norte

Isla
Santa Clara

Punta Freddy

Parque Nacional
Archipiélago de
Juan Fernández

**Playa
del Buque
Varado**

Bahía de la Colonia

Isla Alejandro
Selkirk

**Playa
Larga**

Punta
Negra

0   2.5   5   7.5 km

Punta
Vicente Porras

1 : 250 000

0   2.5   5   7.5 km

1 : 250 000

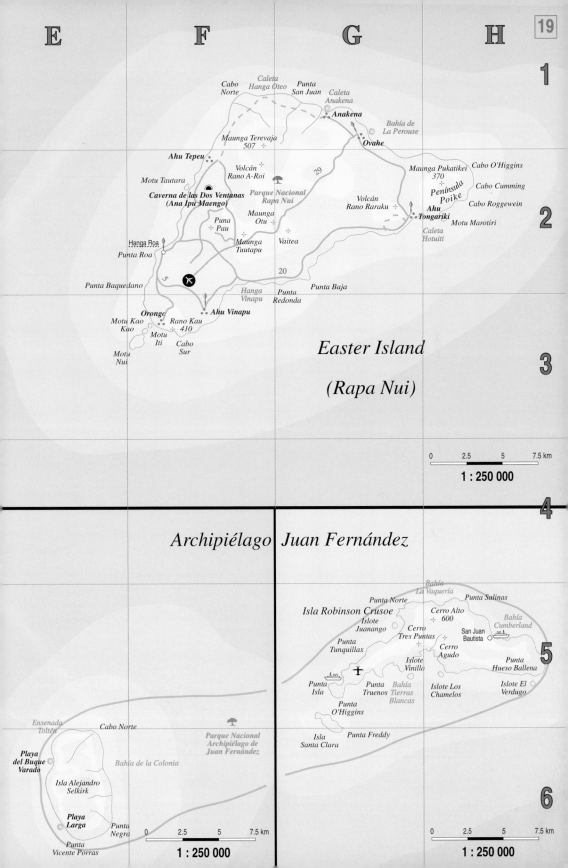

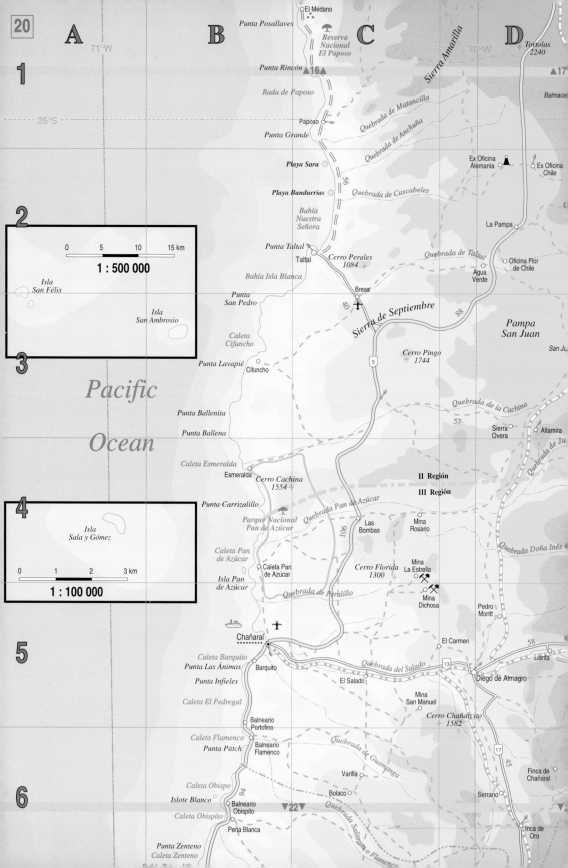

A B C D

1

2

3

4

5

6

71°W

70°W

25°S

Pacific

Ocean

1 : 500 000

0 5 10 15 km

Isla
San Félix

Isla
San Ambrosio

1 : 100 000

0 1 2 3 km

Isla
Sala y Gómez

El Médano
Punta Posallaves
Reserva
Nacional
El Paposo
▲16▲
Punta Rincón
Rada de Paposo
Sierra Amarilla
Tortolas
2240
▲17
Balmace
Paposo
Punta Grande
Quebrada de Matancilla
Quebrada de Anchuña
Ex Oficina
Alemania
▲
Ex Oficina
Chile
Playa Sara
56
Quebrada de Cascabeles
La Pampa
Playa Bandurrias
Bahía
Nuestra
Señora
Punta Taltal
Cerro Perales
1084
Quebrada de Taltal
Oficina Flor
de Chile
Taltal
Agua
Verde
Bahía Isla Blanca
Breas
San Ju
Punta
San Pedro
40
Sierra de Septiembre
88
Pampa
San Juan
Caleta
Cifuncho
Cerro Pingo
1744
Punta Lavapié
Cifuncho
5
Quebrada de la Cachina
Punta Ballenita
57
Sierra
Overa
Altamira
Punta Ballena
Caleta Esmeralda
Esmeralda
Cerro Cachina
1554
II Región
III Región
Punta Carrizalillo
Quebrada Pan de Azúcar
Parque Nacional
Pan de Azúcar
100
Las
Bombas
Mina
Rosario
Caleta Pan
de Azúcar
Caleta Pan
de Azúcar
Cerro Florida
1300
Mina
La Estrella
Isla Pan
de Azúcar
Mina
Dichosa
Pedro
Montt
Quebrada de Peralillo
Chañaral
El Carmen
58
Llanta
Caleta Barquito
Punta Las Ánimas
Barquito
Quebrada del Salado
13
Diego de Almagro
Punta Infieles
El Salado
Caleta El Pedregal
Mina
San Manuel
Balneario
Portofino
Cerro Chañarcito
1582
Caleta Flamenco
Punta Patch
Balneario
Flamenco
Quebrada de Guamanga
17
45
Finca de
Chañaral
Caleta Obispo
Varilla
Islote Blanco
94
Balneario
Obispito
▼22▼
Bolaco
Quebrada Salitrosa o Flamenco
Serrano
Caleta Obispito
Peña Blanca
Inca de
Oro
Punta Zenteno
Caleta Zenteno

E   **F**   **G**   **H**   23

Cerro Pingo
2976

Cerro Ermitaño
6140

Laguna Verde

Paso de
San Francisco
4727 — **1**

Sierra Banderita

Mina La
Coipa

Maricunga

69°W

Cordillera de Claudio Gay

104

Nevado de San Francisco
6018

Quebrada San Andrés

86

Ch 31

▲21▲

Salar de
Maricunga

Parque Nacional
Nevado de Tres Cruces

Nevado de Incahuasi
6621

Laguna Santa
Rosa

Nevado El Fraile
6040

La Puerta

La Cebolla

Quebrada de Paipote

La Junta

Mina
Marte

Nevado de Tres Cruces
6758

Volcán Ojos del Salado
6893

El Volcán

Portezuelo de los Patos
o Cuesta Colorada
4715

2

Río Peladas

Cerro la Ternera
3824

Cerro Azufre o Copiapó
6052

Cerro Nacimiento
6493

Tambería

Quebrada del Patón

Los Azules

Cerro de Monardes
4860

Laguna de la
Salina Verde

P r o v i n c i a
d e
C a t a m a r c a

Cortadera

Salto de
los Mayores

Laguna del
Negro Francisco

Portezuelo de Valle
Ancho Norte
4656

Salina de la
Laguna Verde

RP 45

Cerro Carrizalillo

Río Figueroa

La Guardia

Laguna Verde

Pastos
Largos — **3**

Cerro del Castaño

Volcán Jotabeche
5880

Río Turbio

Portezuelo Vidal Gormaz
4883

CHILE

ARGENTINA

Chaschuil

Río Jorquera

Monte Pissis
6779

Río Pillaguasi

Pastos
Largos

Río Nevado

Las
Empanadas

4

Cerros de Ramada
3620

Río Cachitos

Cerro Bonete
6872

Río de la Troya

Río Pulido

o Estancilla
3550

Paso de Pircas Negras
4166

A r g e n t i n a

Ramadilla

Río Potro

Río Ramadillas

Paso de Peña Negra
4371

de la Iglesia
3940

Río del Medio

Sierra de Peñón

Río Jagüe

Sierra del Toro Negro

5

Cerro El Potro
5830

Río Blanco

Río de Mondosa

Cerro Tronquitos
5740

P r o v i n c i a
d e
S a n   J u a n

Laguna Brava

P r o v i n c i a
d e
L a   R i o j a

Sierra de Vinchina

6

▼25▼

Jagüe

del Rincón
la Flecha
4635

Río Colorado

RP 26

A　　　B　　　C　　　D

1

2

3

4

5

6

29°S

30°S

72°W

Punta Mogote Negro

Bahía Quebrada Honda

Bahía Sarco　　Caleta Sarco

Cabo Bascuñán

▲22▲　　El Sauce

El Morado

Vista Ale

Cabo Leones

Isla Chañaral

Caleta Chañaral

Caleta Chañaral

Bahía Carrizal

Punta Carrizal

Caleta Apolillado

Carrizalillo

III Región

IV Región

Isla Damas

Reserva Nacional
Pingüino de Humboldt

Isla Gaviota

Isla Choros

Los Lobitos

Choros Bajos

Río Los Chor

Bahía Choros

Punta Mar Brava

Isla Chungungo

Cruz Grande

El Tofo

Caleta Totoralillo

Chungungo

Isla Tilgo

La Higuel

200

Islotes Pájaros

Los Hornos

Caleta Los Hornos

Quebrada Ho

Quebrada Honda

Quebrada Las Barran

Caleta Arrayán

El Ror

Punta Poroto

Pacific

Ocean

Teatinos

Punta Teatinos

Juan Soldado

Lamb

Bahía Coquimbo

La Compañía

El Islón

LA SERENA

Ch 41

Alto

Coquimbo

Peñuelas

R

Bahía Herradura de Guayacán

La Herradura

Tierras Blancas

Alg

Totoralillo

Cerrillos

El Peñón

Punta Lagunillas

43

Bahía Guanaquero

Punta Guanaquero

Guanaqueros

Maiten

Bahía Tongoy

Punta Lengua de Vaca

Tongoy

Tambillos

El Cobre

Puerto Aldea

El Peralillo

Las Cardas

Quebrada Tongoicillo

El Tangue

5

Pejerreyes

Punta Farellones

Otárola

Higue

Caleta Totoral de Lengua de Vaca

Pachingo

Panulcillo

Punta Villa Señor

Tolhuán

Recoleta

Los Baños

El Algar

Ensenada Mar Gruesa

Samo Ba

Altos de Talinay

Quebrada de Pachingo

Quebrada Seca

Cerrillos de Tamaya

Guamalata

Punta Talinay

Las Sosas

La Torre

35 Limarí

▼26▼

Trapiche

La Chimba

Oval

Fray Jorge

Río Limarí

37

45

Parque Nacional Fray Jorge

Valle del Encanto

Punta Limarí

Termas de Socos

Chalinga

Camarico Viejo

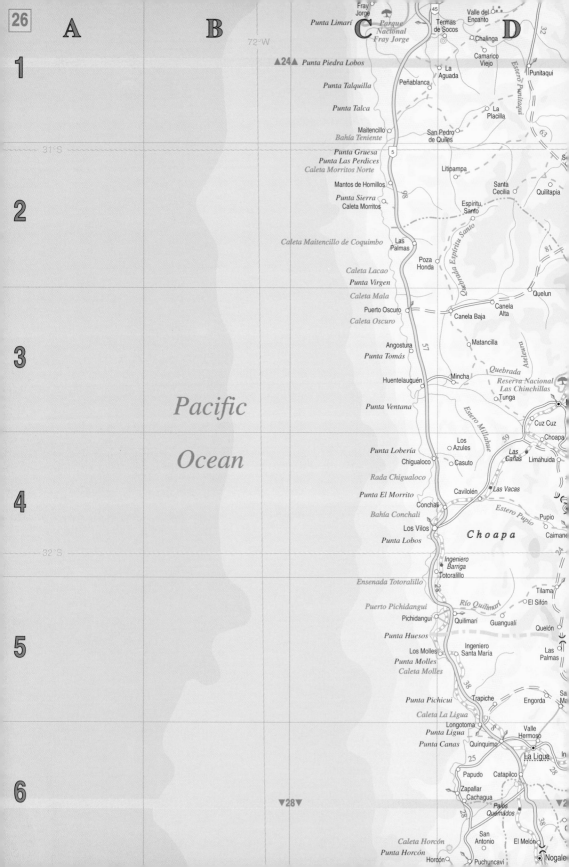

A   B   C   D

1

2

3

4

5

6

Fray Jorge
Punta Limarí
Parque Nacional Fray Jorge
Termas de Socos
Valle del Encanto
32

▲24▲ Punta Piedra Lobos
Peñablanca
La Aguada
Chalinga
Camarico Viejo
Punitaqui
63

Punta Talquilla
La Placilla

Punta Talca

Maitencillo
Bahía Teniente
San Pedro de Quiles

Punta Gruesa
Punta Las Perdices
Caleta Morritos Norte
5
Litipampa
Santa Cecilia
Quilitapia

Mantos de Hornillos
Punta Sierra
Caleta Morritos
Espíritu Santo

Caleta Maitencillo de Coquimbo
Las Palmas
98

Caleta Lacao
Punta Virgen
Poza Honda
Quelun
81

Caleta Mala
Puerto Oscuro
Caleta Oscuro
Canela Baja
Canela Alta

Angostura
Punta Tomás
Matancilla
57

Huentelauquén
Mincha
Quebrada

Reserva Nacional Las Chinchillas
Tunga

Pacific
Punta Ventana
Estero Millahue
Cuz Cuz

Ocean
Los Azules
Choapa
59

Punta Lobería
Chigualoco
Casuto
Las Cañas
Limáhuida

Rada Chigualoco

Punta El Morrito
Cavilolén
Las Vacas

Conchalí
Bahía Conchalí
Estero Pupio
Pupio

Los Vilos
Punta Lobos
Choapa
Caimane

Ensenada Totoralillo
Ingeniero Barriga
Totoralillo
Tilama

Puerto Pichidangui
Pichidangui
Río Quilimarí
El Sifón

Quilimarí
Guanguali
Quelón

Punta Huesos
Ingeniero Santa María
Las Palmas

Los Molles
Punta Molles
Caleta Molles
38

Punta Pichicui
Trapiche
Engorda
Sa Ma

Caleta La Ligua
Longotoma
8

Punta Ligua
Quinquimo
Valle Hermoso

Punta Canas
La Ligua
28

25

Papudo
Catapilco

Zapallar
Cachagua
Palos Quemados

▼28▼
28
38

Caleta Horcón
San Antonio
El Melón

Punta Horcón
Nogale

Horcón
Puchuncaví

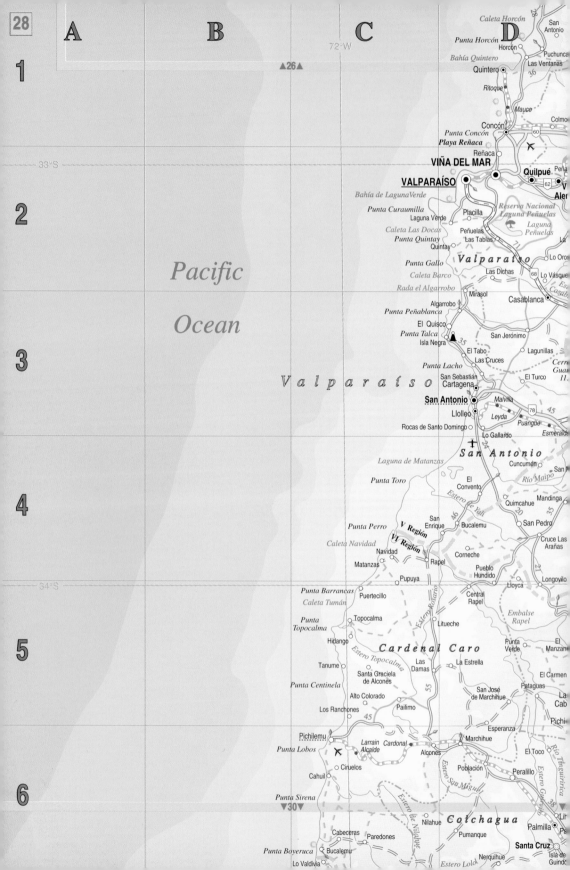

A   B   C   D

1

72°W

▲26▲

Caleta Horcón
Punta Horcón
San Antonio
Puchuncaví
Horcón
Bahía Quintero
Las Ventanas
Quintero
36
Ritoque
Mauco
Colmo
Concón
60
Punta Concón
Playa Reñaca
Reñaca
Peña
VIÑA DEL MAR
Quilpué
Aler
62
V
VALPARAÍSO

2

33°S

Bahía de LagunaVerde
Reñaca
Reserva Nacional
Laguna Peñuelas
Punta Curaumilla
Placilla
Laguna
Peñuelas
Laguna Verde
Peñuelas
La
Caleta Las Docas
Las Tablas
71
Punta Quintay
Valparaíso
Lo Oros
Quintay
Lo Vásque
Las Dichas
68
Punta Gallo
Caleta Barco
Casablanca
Rada el Algarrobo
Mirasol
Es
Casab
Algarrobo
Punta Peñablanca
El Quisco
San Jerónimo
Punta Talca
35
Lagunillas
Isla Negra
El Tabo
Cerro
Valparaíso
Las Cruces
Gua
11.
Punta Lacho
El Turco
San Sebastián
Cartagena
San Antonio
Malvilla
Llolleo
Leyda
78
45
Rocas de Santo Domingo
Puangue
Lo Gallardo
Esmerald

3

Pacific

Ocean

4

San Antonio
Cuncumén
San
Laguna de Matanzas
Río Maipo
Punta Toro
El
Convento
Estero de Yali
Quimcahue
Mandinga
V Región
San
Enrique
Bucalemu
San Pedro
20
35
Punta Perro
VI Región
Cruce Las
Arañas
Caleta Navidad
Corneche
Navidad
Pueblo
Hundido
Longovilo
Matanzas
Rapel
Pupuya
Lloyca

5

34°S

Punta Barrancas
Central
Rapel
Caleta Tumán
Puertecillo
Estero Rosario
Lituche
Punta
Topocalma
Topocalma
Embalse
Rapel
Hidango
Cardenal Caro
Punta
Verde
El
Manzan
Tanume
Las
Damas
La Estrella
55
El Carmen
Santa Graciela
de Alcones
Punta Centinela
San José
de Marchihue
Pataguas
Alto Colorado
La
Cab
Los Ranchones
Pailimo
45
Pichi
Esperanza
Pichilemu
Marchihue
Larraín
Alcalde
Cardonal
El Toco
Punta Lobos
Alcones
Peralillo
Ciruelos
Población

6

Cahuil
Estero San Miguel
Punta Sirena
▼30▼
Estero de Nilahue
Colchagua
Li
Cabeceras
Paredones
Pumanque
Palmilla
Punta Boyeruca
Bucalemu
Nerquihue
Santa Cruz
Isla de
Lo Valdivia
Estero Lolol
Guind

A   B   C   D

74°W

1

73°W

Cautín

Río Cholchol   Cholchol   Pillanlelbún

Trovolhue   52   Ranquilco   Nueva   Cajón

▲32▲   Imperial

Nehuentué   Carahue   Boroa   Prat   **TEMU**

Puerto Saavedra   Río Cautín   Almagro   35   ✈

Boca Budi   Metrenco

Puerto   Quepe

Punta Puaucho   Domínguez

21

Martínez   Freire

Laguna   Barros   de Rosas

Budi   Teodoro   Arana   Pitrufquén

Schmidt

2

39°S

Río Toltén   Comuy   Gorbea

Gualpín   Quinque   Quitratue

Nueva   Lastarria

Toltén   Afquintué

Toltén   *Cordillera de*

Punta Nihue   *Mahuicanchi*   Loncoche

Cerro de   IX Región   15

Bahía Queule   *Puralaco 792*   X Región   La Paz

3   *Punta Ronca*   Queule   Lanco   Salto

Bahía Maiquillahue   28   Puringue   del Agua   Ch

Punta Maiquillahue   Mehuin   Purulón   203

22   51

Punta Chanchán   San José de   Los

la Mariquina   Tallos

Mariquina

Cruces   12   Máfil   *Río Iñaque*   Dollinc

Punta Rocura   Curiñanco   Puerto   62

Altué   Río Pichoy   Pucono

Ch   *Río Máfil*

205   Huellelhue   Quinchilca

4   **VALDIVIA**   Antilhué   *Purey*   Folilco

Niebla   Pishuinco   30   Los

16   Lagos

Amargos   *Río Valdivia*   *Lipingue*   Huite

Corral   Ch   30   56

Caleta Chaihuin   207   Reumén   Dol

35

Punta Galera   *Río Chaihuin*   Los Ulmos   Paillaco   *Río Lollehue*

40°S   La Peña

Punta Colún   *Monumento Natural*   Pichirropulli

Alerce Costero

5   *Punta Hueicolla*   Catamutún   Los   Puerto

Hueicolla   El Mirador   Conales   Nuevo

Caleta Lameguapi   Llancacura   Rapaco

La Barra   *Río Bueno*   Cudico   Quilaico

Traiguén   La Unión

Caleta Milagro   Trinidad   Río Bueno   *Río Trani*

Lago   Junta   Trumao   Empalme   Guzmán   Vivanco

Trinidad   *Río Chaicí*

Quilacáhuin   San Pablo   Trapi

Punta Pucatrihue   Caracol   El Crucero

Bellavista   Chacayal   Purrapel

6   El Hoble   30   Remehué   *Río Chirri*

Misión de San   59

Pucatrihue   Juan de la Costa   *Río Pilmaiquén*

▼36▼   48

Río Contaco   Cunamo   Las Lumas   Chirre

Bahía Mansa   Puaucho   35   ✕

Caleta Maicolpué   Maicolpué   Contaco   **OSORNO**   Las Quemas   *Río Damas*   Nueva   Entre

Punta Llesquehue   *Osorno*   Pichil   Esperanza   Lagos

5

Millantue

Pacific

Ocean

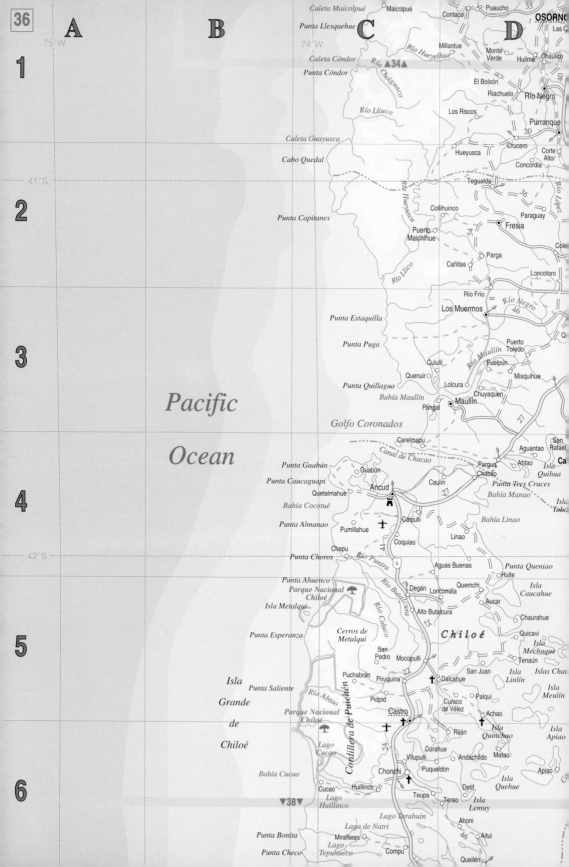

A　　　B　　　C　　　D

1

2

3

4

5

6

75°W

41°S

42°S

74°W

Pacific

Ocean

Caleta Maicolpué
Maicolpué
Contaco
Puaucho
35
OSORNO
Punta Llesquehue
Las C
Río Hueyelhue
Millantue
Monte
Verde
Huilma
Chaulinc
Caleta Cóndor
Río Chelguaco
▲34▲
Punta Cóndor
El Bolsón
Riachuelo
Río Negro
Río Lliuco
Los Riscos
Purranque
20
Caleta Guayusca
Hueyusca
Crucero
Corte
Alto
Cabo Quedal
Concordia
Tegualda
36
Punta Capitanes
Collihuinco
Paraguay
Río Hueyusca
Puerto
Maichihue
34
Fresia
Cole
Parga
Cañitas
Loncotoro
Río Llico
Río Frío
Río Negro
46
Punta Estaquilla
Los Muermos
Punta Puga
Puerto
Toledo
Río Maullín
Puelpún
Cululil
Quenuir
Misquihue
Punta Quillagua
Lolcura
Chuyaquen
27
Bahía Maullín
Maullín
Pangal
Golfo Coronados
San
Rafael
Carelmapu
Aguantao
Abtao
Ca
Punta Guabún
Canal de Chacao
Pargua
Isla
Guabún
Chacáo
Quihua
Punta Caucaguapi
Punta Tres Cruces
Quetalmahue
Caulín
27
Bahía Manao
Ancud
Isla
Taba
Bahía Cocotué
Caipulli
Bahía Linao
Punta Almanao
Pumillahue
Linao
Coquiao
Chepu
Río Puntra
Punta Choros
5
Aguas Buenas
Punta Queniao
Punta Ahuenco
Degán
Quemchi
Huite
Parque Nacional
Chiloé
Loncomilla
Isla
Caucahue
Río Butalcura
Isla Metalqui
Aucar
Alto Butalcura
Chaurahue
Río Coluco
25
Quicavi
Cerros de
Metalqui
Chiloé
Punta Esperanza
San
Pedro
Mocopulli
Tenaún
Isla
Mechuque
Puchabrán
San Juan
Isla
Islas Chau
Punta Saliente
Piruquina
Dalcahue
Linlín
Isla
Grande
Río Abtao
Pidpid
Palqui
Meulín
Parque Nacional
Chiloé
Curaco
de Vélez
Achao
de
Castro
Rilán
Isla
Apiao
Isla
Quinchao
Chiloé
Curahue
Isla
Apiao
Lago
Cucao
Vilupulli
Andachildo
Matao
Apiao
Chonchi
Puqueldón
Bahía Cucao
Cucao
Huillinco
Teupa
Detif
Isla
Quehue
▼38▼
Lago
Huillinco
Terao
Isla
Lemuy
Lago Tarahuin
Ahoni
Lago de Natri
46
Punta Bonita
Miraflores
Compu
Aitui
Lago
Tepuhueco
Queilén
Punta Checo

Cordillera de Piuchén
Isla
de
Chiloé

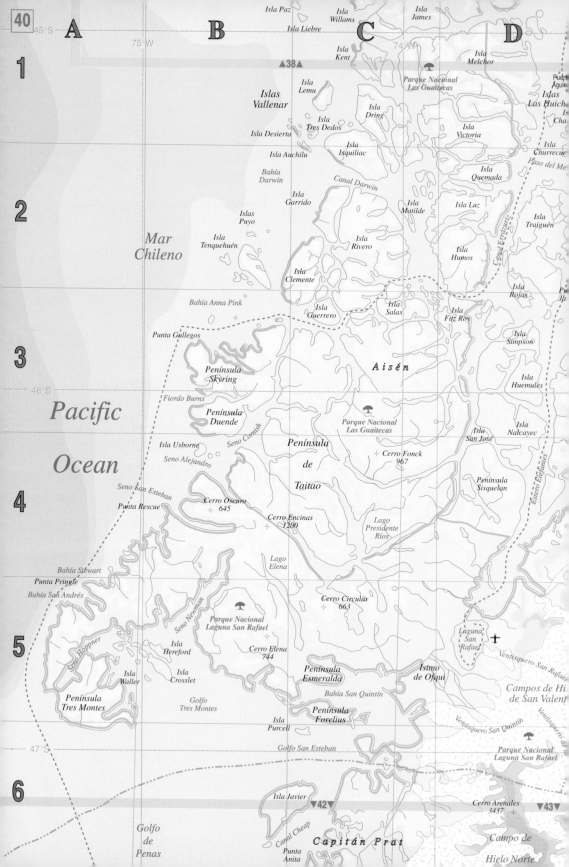

Cerro Maca
2958

▲38▲

Lago Yulton

Lago Meullin

73°W

Lago Presidente Roosevelt

Río Mañihuales

▲39▲

Mañihuales

72°W

Mina El Toqui

Katterfeld

1

Lago de los Palos

Río Cañon

27

30

Cerro Colorado 1850

53

Baño Nuevo

Lago Coyte

Seno Aisén

Lago Largo

Villa Ortega

Nirehuao

Lago Pampa Alta

Puerto Aisén

Ch 240

35

37

Cerro la Gloria 1920

36

49

Ch 240

Coihaique Alto

Paso Coihaique

2

Lago Cóndor

Puerto Chacabuco

Lago Portales

Parque Nacional Río Simpson

Salto de la Virgen

Coihaique

Bellavista

Lago Riesco

Reserva Nacional Coihaique

Monumento Natural Dos Lagunas

RN 26

Alto Río Mayo

Lago Zenteno

Lago Castor

Termas de Quitralco

Volcán Cóndor 1830

Cerro Divisadero 1552

Cerro La Bandera 1013

Lago Claro

Lago Ellis

Lago Elizalde

Cerro Iglesias 1835

41

Lago Pollux

Argentina

Río Huemules

Cerro Hudson

Lago Caro

Elizalde

Río Simpson

Ch 245

17

Lago Blanco

RP 35

3

Coihaique

Lago La Paloma

Reserva Nacional Cerro Castillo

12

11

Balmaceda

Valle Huemules

CHILE

ARGENTINA

Lago Guenguel

Cerro Campana 2027

Río Ibáñez

Villa Cerro Castillo

30

20

Portezuelo Huemules

Río Guenguel

7

122

Lago Lapparent

El Portezuelo

Río Fénix Grande

Cerro Redondo 1842

Puerto Ingeniero Ibáñez

Bahía Ibáñez

Ingeniero Pallavicini

RP 45

4

Lago Bayo

Puerto Murta

Puerto Cristal

Puerto Avellanos

Bahía Jara

Lago Verde

Lago Buenos Aires

Monte San Valentín o San Clemente 3910

Puerto Sánchez

82

Chile Chico

Los Antiguos

74

RP 43

5

Puerto Río Tranquilo

49

Lago General Carrera

Puerto Fachinal

Río de las Nieves

Ch 205

Mallín Grande

Isla Macías

General Carrera

Reserva Nacional Lago Jeinimem

Lago Jeiniment

Cerro Cumbre Rojiza 1407

Puerto Guadal

El Maitén

Lago Bertrand

53

Lago del Sello

Puerto Bertrand

▼43▼

Valle Chacabuco

Río Chacabuco

74

Cerro Baker 2230

Río Ecker

Cerro Tres Picos 1900

Río Nef

Río Baker

17

Reserva Nacional Lago Cochrane

Lago Cochrane

Paso Rodolfo Roballos 655

RP 41

6

A   B   C   D

76°W   75°W   74°W

1

2

3

4

5

6

Isla Javier

Canal Cheap

Punta
Anita

▲40▲   Golfo
de
Penas

*Parque Nacional
Laguna San Rafael*

Cerro Stokes
800

Cerro Triángulo
880

Boca de
Canales

Seno Pulpo

Isla
Ayautau

*Península
Larenas*

Archipiélago Guayaneco

Bahía Harvey

Isla
San Pedro

*Reserva Nacional
Katalalixar*

Pacific

Isla
Wager

*Bahía
Tarn*

Isla
Sombrero

Isla
Vicente

Capitán Prat

Isla
Byron

Isla
Zealous

Isla
Porcia

48°S

Ocean

Paso Suroeste

Islas
Jungfrauen

Isla
Juan Stuven

Isla
Scout

Isla
Orlebar

Isla
Merino Jarpa

Isla
Millar

Canal Baker

Isla Breaksea

Isla Blanca

**Península
Swett**

Canal Barbarrosa

Punta Dora

Cerro Cerrucho
785

Reserva Nacional
Katalalixar

Isla
Schlucht

Península Negra

Isla
Van der
Meulen

Punta Roth

Cerro Roth
600

Isla
Prat

*Parque Nacional
Bernardo O'Higgins*

Canal Fallos

Isla
Campana

Canal Albatros

Isla
Caldcleugh

Isla
Ofhidro

Canal Octubre

Isla
Middle

Isla
Farquhar

Isla
Little
Wellington

Isla
Hillyar

Isla
Boxer

Canal Farquhar

Cerro Mediterrá
1737

Isla
Patricio
Lynch

XI Región

Canal Adalberto

Isla
Williams

Punta Conglomerada

Isla
Riquelme

XII Región

Isla
Knor

*Bahía
Tribune*

Isla
Cabrales

Isla
Aldea

Canal Castillo

Isla
Videla

Bahía
Dineley

Isla
Orella

Cerro
Walkyrenstein
945

Isla
Wellington

49°S

Punta Dineley

Isla
Esmeralda

Última Esperanza

Magallanes

▼44▼

Isla
Covadonga

Isla
Stosch

*Parque Nacional
Bernardo O'Higgins*

Isla
Angamos

Puerto
Edén

Isla Carlos

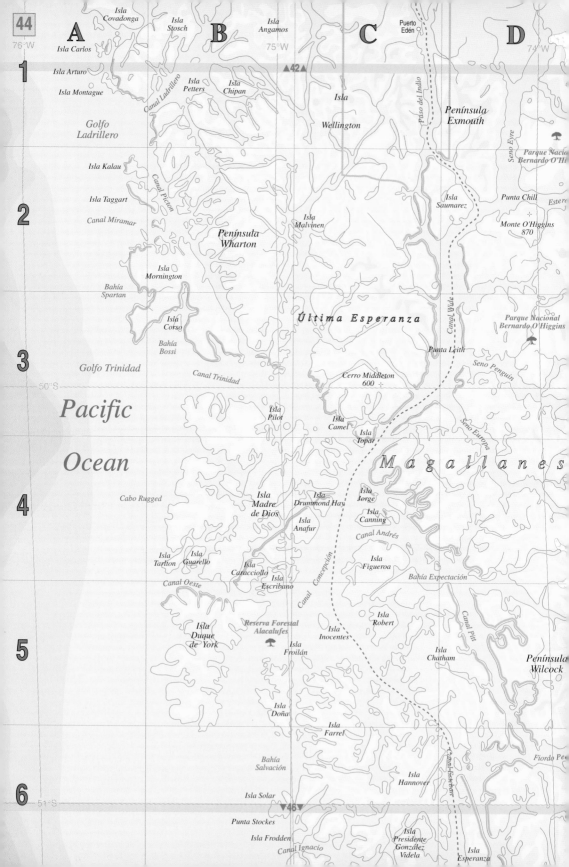

76°W

A

B

75°W

C

Puerto
Edén

D

74°W

1

Isla
Covadonga

Isla
Stosch

Isla
Angamos

Isla Carlos

Isla Arturo

▲42▲

Isla Montague

Canal Ladrillero

Isla
Petters

Isla
Chipan

Isla

Wellington

Paso del Indio

Península
Exmouth

Seno Eyre

Parque Nacio
Bernardo O'Hi

Golfo
Ladrillero

2

Isla Kalau

Canal Picton

Isla Taggart

Canal Miramar

Península
Wharton

Isla
Malvinen

Isla
Saumarez

Punta Chill

Monte O'Higgins
870

Ester

Isla
Mornington

Bahía
Spartan

Última Esperanza

Parque Nacional
Bernardo O'Higgins

3

Isla
Corso

Bahía
Bossi

Punta Leith

Seno Penguin

50°S

Golfo Trinidad

Canal Trinidad

Cerro Middleton
600 ✛

Pacific

Isla
Pilot

Isla
Camel

Isla
Topar

Seno Europa

Ocean

M a g a l l a n e s

Cabo Rugged

Isla
Madre
de Dios

Isla
Drummond Hay

Isla
Jorge

4

Isla
Anafur

Isla
Canning

Canal Andrés

Isla
Tarlton

Isla
Guarello

Isla
Caracciollo

Isla
Escribano

Canal Concepción

Isla
Figueroa

Bahía Expectación

Canal Pitt

Canal Oeste

Isla
Duque
de York

Reserva Forestal
Alacalufes

Isla
Inocentes

Isla
Robert

5

Isla
Froilán

Isla
Chatham

Península
Wilcock

Isla
Doña

Isla
Farrel

Canal Esteban

Bahía
Salvación

Isla
Hannover

Fiordo Pe

6

51°S

Isla Solar

▼46▼

Punta Stockes

Isla Frodden

Canal Ignacio

Isla
Presidente
González
Videla

Isla
Esperanza

Lago Tar
RP 31
72° W

1

Campo de

Hielo Sur

▲43▲

Río Potranca

Monte Chaltel
o Fitz Roy
3406

El
Chalten

Estancia
San José

Laguna
La Rubia

Cerro Huemul
2877

Estancia
Punta del Lago

2

RP 23

Lago Viedma

Punta del
Lago

RN 40

Cerro Norte
2950

Río Cóndor

Cerro Indice
829

Parque Nacional
Los Glaciares

Lago
Viedma

CHILE

ARGENTINA

Río Cuanaco

3

Lago
Tannhauser

98

Estancia
La Blanca

Cerro Bertrand
3270

Argentina

RP 19

Cerro Bolados
2940

Lago
Grande

Brazo Norte

Estancia
San Ernesto

Lago
Argentino

Cerro Negro
1650

35

Río Bote

4

Península
Avellaneda

RP 11

El Calafate

RN 40

Canal de los Témpanos

Punta
Bandera

RP 8

Río Bote

Península
Magallanes

Lago
Sarmiento

Parque Nacional
Bernardo O'Higgins

RP 11

Estancia
Lago Roca

El
Centinela

Fiordo Asia

Estancia
Lago Rico

Paso Portezuelo Baguales IV
1271

Brazo Sur

Paso Portezuelo Baguales I
704

5

Lago
Roca

Cerro Obelisco
1614

RN 40

Ventisquero Grey

Cerro Daudet
1770

Río Zamora

Estancia
Las Chinas

Cerro Blanco
1910

Lago
Dickson

Laguna
Azul

Lago
Dulcinea

Parque Nacional
Torres del Paine

Cordillera de Paine

Laguna
Amarga

Lago
Palique

6

Cerro Paine Grande
2730

▲47▲

Lago
Nordenskjöld

Lago
Sarmiento

124

Lago
Grey

RN 40

9

Lago
Tapo Aike

A   B   C   D

75°W   74°W

1

2

3

4

5

6

Isla Frodden

Isla Hannover

Canal Ignacio

Isla Caballo Blanco

Isla Valenzuela

Isla Armonía

Isla Presidente González Videla

Isla Esperanza

▲44▲

Isla Dagnino

Punta Huemul

Isla Agustín

Isla Jorge Montt

Isla Evans

Grupo Solari

Isla Vancouver

Ensenada San Blas

Isla Diego de Almagro

Isla Virtudes

Isla Daroch

Canal Castro

Grupo Carmela

Paso Tarleton

Canal Sarmiento

Isla Carr

Grupo Lobos

Isla Angelotti

Grupo Gómez Carreño

2

Estrecho Nelson

Última Esperanza

Isla Piazzi

Isla Ramírez

Canal Smith

3

Isla Vidal Gormaz

Canal Uribe

Islas Rennell

52°S

Isla Contreras

Isla Maldonado

Canal Cutler

Pacific

Isla Bordes

Isla Barros Arana

Isla Silva Renard

Ocean

Reserva Nacional Alacalufes

Islas Chaigneau

4

Golfo Sarmiento de Gamboa

Isla Pacheco

Isla Rosas

Isla Juan Guillermos

Isla Djenana

Isla King

Islotes Evangelistas

Canal Esmeralda

Grupo Theo

Archipiélago Reina Adelaida

Isla Ye Bu

Grupo Narborough

Isla Cóndor

Isla Freire

5

Isla Staveley

Isla Latorre

Isla Parker

Bahía Parker

Estrecho de Magallanes

Canal

Puerto Misericordia

6

Caleta Mataura

▼50▼

Isla Desolación

53°S

Puerto Churruca

1

Lago Sarmiento

Lago Grey

Parque Nacional Torres del Paine

737W

▲45▲

Cerro Donoso ÷ 1460

Sección Lazo Balseo

Lago del Toro

Estancia Kark

Cerro Castillo

Cancha Carrera

Laguna Esperanza

RN 40

Lago Tyndall

Lago Brach

Cerro Balmaceda 2035 ÷

Puerto Toro

Sierra Arturo Prat

Lago Porteño

Sierra Dorotea

Hotel Tres Pasos

Argentina

2

Seno Última Esperanza

Parque Nacional Bernardo O'Higgins

Lago Sofía

63

nsula aines

Península Antonio Varas

Río Turbio

J Dufour

Dorotea

Cordillera Sarmiento de Gamboa

Seno de las Montañas

Monumento Natural Cueva del Milodón

Puerto Bories

El Turbio

Estancia Punta Alta

RN 40

88

Península Roca

Puerto Natales

Estancia Río Tranquilo

Laguna Cóndor

3

Isla Newton

Reserva Nacional Alacalufes

Golfo Almirante Montt

Lago Balmaceda

Lago Diana

Laguna Larga

ARGENTINA

Península Barros Arana

Lago Anibal Pinto

9

CHILE

Península Zach

Seno Unión

La Junta

115

Hotel Río Rubens

ARGENTINA

4

Península Zach

Kerber

Santa Teresita

Río Peniente

44

María Sofía

Magallanes

Río Blanco

Cordillera Pinto

Cordillera Vidal

Península Muñoz Gamero

Puerto Hewett

Cerro La Silueta ÷ 1285

Estancia Verano

nuel iguez

Magallanes

Puerto Altamirano

5

Puerto Arturo

Cerro Diadema 1238

Seno Skyring

Río Verde

Puerto Cascada

Estancia Ponsonby

Isla Caldera

Canal Euston

Estancia Rocallosa

Isla Zañartu

Cerro Atalaya 1830

Isla Grande

Cordillera Serrucho

Bahía aufort

Laguna Riesco

Cordillera Riesco

Cerro Pirámide 1200

Vaquería

6

▼50▼

Isla Providencia

▼51▼

Isla Riesco

Estancia Invierno

Estrecho de Magallanes

Reserva Nacional Alacalufes

Seno Otway

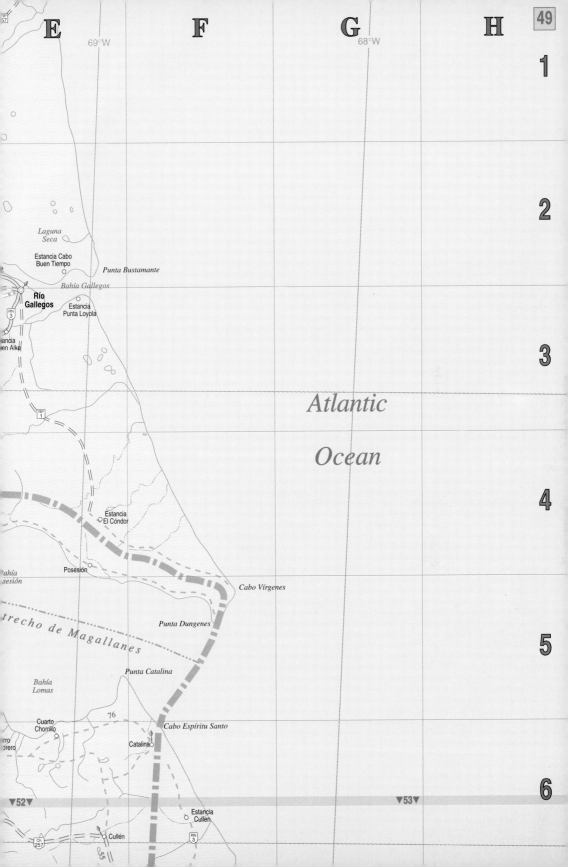

69°W

68°W

1

2

Laguna Seca

Estancia Cabo
Buen Tiempo

Punta Bustamante

Bahía Gallegos

Río Gallegos

RN 3

Estancia
Punta Loyola

ancia
en Aike

3

Atlantic

RP 1

Ocean

4

Estancia
El Cóndor

ahía
sesión

Posesión

Cabo Vírgenes

trecho de Magallanes

Punta Dungenes

5

Punta Catalina

Bahía Lomas

76

Cuarto
Chorrillo

Cabo Espíritu Santo

rro
orero

Catalina

6

Estancia
Cullén

Ch 257

RN 3

Cullén

55

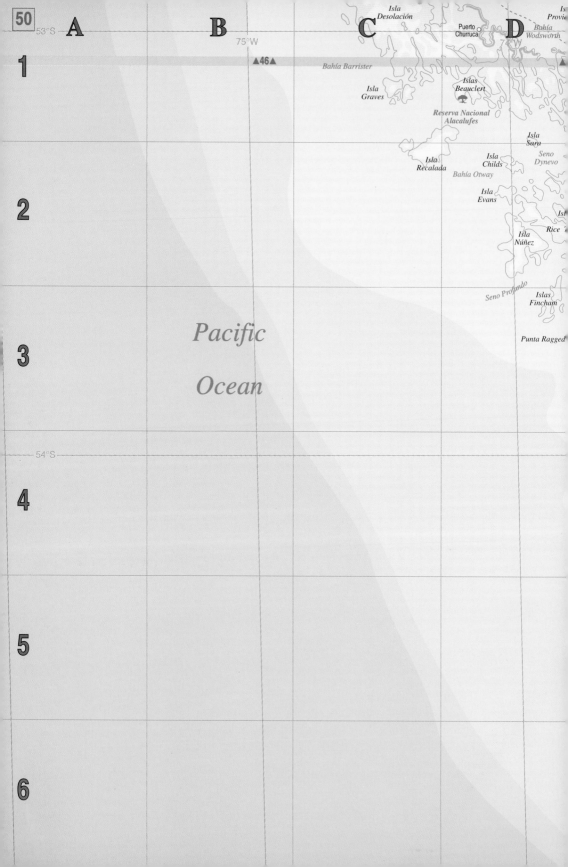

53°S

A   **B**   **C**   **D**

75°W

1   ▲46▲   *Bahía Barrister*

Isla Desolación

Puerto Churruca

Bahía Wodsworth

Is Pro

Isla Graves

Islas Beauclert

Reserva Nacional Alacalufes

Isla Sara

Isla Recalada   *Isla Childs*   *Seno Dynevo*

Bahía Otway

Isla Evans

Is
Rice

2

Isla Núñez

Seno Profundo   *Islas Fincham*

Punta Ragged

3   *Pacific*

Ocean

54°S

4

5

6

Estancia
Invierno

Seno Otway

▲47▲

72°W

1

Punta Sunshine

Río Canelos

▲48▲

Golfo
Xaultegua

Punta Villiers

Reserva Nacional
Magallanes

73°W

Península

Monte Muela
÷ 1189

Córdoba

Reserva Forestal
Lago Varillar

Reserva Nacional
Alacalufes

2

Península
de
Brunswick

M a g a l l a n e s

Cerro Valenzuela
985

Península
Ulloa

Isla
Carlos III

Cerro Tres Picos
÷ 1200

Isla

Estrecho de Magallanes

3

Santa Inés

M a g a l l a n e s

Paso Inglés

Isla
Cayetano

Cabo
Froward

Wakefield

▼52▼

Isla
Carlos

Isla
Clarence

Península
Greenough

Isla
James

Isla
Libertad

Canal Barbara

4

Islas
Crafton

Bahía
Stokes

Isla
Guardián
Brito

Seno
Dyneley

Isla
Capitán Aracena

Isla
Ilabella

Isla
Lort

Isla
Stanley

Isla
Diego

Islas
Agnes

Paso Aviador Ibáñez

Isla
Mortimer

Isla
Kempe

Isla
Skyring

Canal Cockburn

Islas
Magill

Isla
Furia

Parque Nacional
Alberto de Agostini

5

Isla Noir

Isla
Aguirre

Península Brecknock

Isla
London

Grupo
Camden

Isla
Sidney

Isla
Basket

6

Bahía
Stewart

Isla
Stewart

Islas Gilbert

A **B** **C** **D**

53°S

71°W

1

Mina Carbón Peket

✈

Río Seco

9

Bahía Gente Grande

Estancia Sarita

Laguna Deseada

▲48▲

Río Oro

Río Oscar

Río O'Higgins

▲49▲

50

Reserva Nacional Magallanes

Mina Loreto

✝ PUNTA ARENAS

Estrecho de Magallanes

Paso Nuevo

Laguna Serrano

Monumento Natural Laguna de los Cisnes

Laguna Verde

Río China Creek

China Creek

La Bel

Porvenir

Laguna de Los Cisnes

Puerto Nuevo

Laguna Vergara

43

Estancia Guairabo

Bahía Porvenir

Estancia Dalmacia

Antonia

58

Bahía Agua Fresca

2

Punta Santa María

Paso Boquerón

Caleta Esperanza

Onaisin

Laguna Ema

Río San Juan

Agua Fresca

Bahía Inútil

Río Chi

Río Amarillo

▲ Fuerte Bulnes

Punta San Juan

Punta Camerón

Camerón

Río Zapato

Río Japón

Estancia Russfin

Cerro Graves 462

Timaukel

Canal Whiteside

3

Magallanes

Cabo San Isidro

Puerto Almeida

Magallanes

Isla Grande de Tierra del Fuego

Estancia Río Grand

Puerto San Antonio

Puerto Yartou

Cabo Froward

Isla Dawson

Seno Owen

Río Cóndor

Lago Lynch

▼51▼

54°S

Seno Magdalena

Puerto Hope

Isla Vickham

Puerto Arturo

Tierra del Fuego

Lago Chico

Lago Blanco

4

Isla Capitán Aracena

Seno Brenton

Canal Magdalena

Cabo Expectación

Seno Almirantazgo

Bahía Filton

Bahía Brookes

Cerro Seymour 1057

Seno Keats

Seno Agostini

5

Península Rolando

Parque Nacional Alberto de Agostini

Cordillera Darwin

Sierra de Valdiv

Cerro Mayo 1798

Cerro Darwin 2430

Antártica Chilena

Cerro Italia 2350

Canal Ballenero

6

Isla Stewart

Isla O'Brien

▼54▼

Seno Darwin

Islas Gilbert

Isla Londonderry

Isla Cook

Isla Darwin

Isla Thompson

Isla Gordon

Getting Around Chile & Easter Island

Bus

Chilean long-distance buses are fast, modern, comfortable and reasonably priced – one of the longest trips in the country, the 2050 km from Arica to Santiago, costs around US$50 in the peak summer season. Fares differ among companies, and promotions (*ofertas*) can reduce normal fares by half. Reservations are generally not essential, but are a good idea in the summer peak season (from Christmas to the end of February), around Semana Santa (Easter), and around mid-September's patriotic holidays.

Ordinary buses are comfortable enough, but on the longer runs, sleeper *(salón cama)* buses offer extra leg room and reclining seats with calf-rests and footrests; fares are about 50% higher than other services. Smoking is prohibited on buses throughout the country.

On secondary routes, buses are older, more basic and less frequent (or even non-existent in more remote areas). These *micros*, which sometimes lack reclining seats, may be packed with locals and their produce.

Train

Passenger rail services are very limited. The only long-distance routes are from Santiago's Estación Central south to Chillán, Concepción, Temuco and intermediates (continuing to Puerto Varas in summer only). There's a sporadic narrow-gauge spur line from Talca to Constitución, and commuter lines run from Santiago south to Rancagua and from Valparaíso/Viña del Mar east to Villa Alemana and Limache.

Long-distance trains have three classes: *económica*, *salón* and *dormitorio* (sleeper). The sleeper class is divided into *cama alta* (upper bunk) and the more expensive *cama baja* (lower bunk). On the 20-hour trip from Santiago to Puerto Varas, the longest run in the country, fares are approximately US$21 *económica*, US$35 *salón*, US$44 *cama alta*, and US$60 *cama baja*.

Road

Chile's public transport system is extensive, but many of the country's most interesting features are accessible by motor vehicle only. The main north-south highways are generally paved and in good condition, with the exception of the famous Camino Austral south of Puerto Montt, but most roads into the Andean foothills and cordillera have gravel or dirt surfaces. Some of these are excellent, while others are in very poor condition; before making extensive excursions into areas like the northern altiplano, try to verify road conditions and determine whether recent rains may have made some areas impassable. Bridges may be non-existent, necessitating stream fords, and 4WD may be necessary to negotiate muddy areas.

Car rental has become increasingly expensive, often ranging upwards of US$100 per day for popular *doble cabina* (double-seated) Japanese pickup trucks without 4WD. Extended rentals, a week or longer, can be relatively economical for groups. Chile's reservoir of used cars has made purchase an increasingly attractive option for visitors, but prices are still higher than for

Volcán Osorno, Lago Llanquihue

WAYNE BERNHARDSON

corresponding vehicles in Europe or North America.

Operating a car in Chile is much cheaper than in Europe but dearer than in North America; the price of *bencina* (petrol) is about US$0.55 per litre, that of *gas-oil* (diesel) significantly cheaper. Away from the main paved highways, carry extra fuel.

Drivers of any vehicle should carry all relevant documents, including proof of ownership, insurance and an International Driving Permit (available from a motoring organisation in your own country).

Bicycle

Bicycle touring is an increasingly popular way of getting around Chile, especially in the southern lake region and along the Camino Austral. Because only the main longitudinal highways are paved, and even those often have narrow unpaved shoulders, most long-distance cyclists prefer mountain bikes. Rental bikes are readily available at reasonable prices in heavily touristed areas, and bike repair facilities are common, though in some out-of-the-way places spares may be limited.

Boat

In southern archipelagic Chile, from Puerto Montt southward, scenic ferry services are common – one of the country's most appealing and popular trips is the four-day, three-night cruise from Puerto Montt to Puerto Natales. The ferry cruise from Puerto Montt or Puerto Chacabuco to Parque Nacional Laguna San Rafael and the combination boat-bus excursion across Lago Todos Los Santos to Bariloche, Argentina, are also major attractions. Shorter ferry services, such as those in and around the Isla Grande de Chiloé, are primarily for transport, but still very enjoyable.

With the exception of the passenger ferry from Punta Arenas to Porvenir, only luxury cruises ply the most southerly routes along the Estrecho de Magallanes (Strait of Magellan).

Easter Island

There is no formal public transportation on Rapa Nui, but walking and rented horses, mountain bikes, motorbikes and cars are all reasonable options. Walking is only recommended for sites near Hanga Roa because of the scarcity of water.

The standard rental period for all forms of transportation is the eight-hour day, though it's possible to arrange overnight rentals. Typical rental fees are US$13 for mountain bikes, US$15 for horses, US$35 for an ordinary passenger car, and US$50 for a 4WD vehicle. Some areas off the main island circuit, which is very good and may soon be paved, would be easier with a 4WD vehicle.

WAYNE BERNHARDSON

Colourful fishing boats, Ancud, Isla Grande de Chiloé

Comment Circuler au Chili et à l'Île de Pâques

Bus

Au Chili, les bus interurbains sont rapides, modernes, confortables et relativement bon marché – l'un des trajets les plus longs que l'on puisse faire dans le pays, entre Arica et Santiago (2 050 km), coûte environ 250 FF en pleine saison. Les tarifs varient selon les compagnies et certaines promotions (*ofertas*) réduisent les prix de moitié. Il n'est généralement pas indispensable de réserver, mais cela est tout de même préférable durant l'été (de Noël à la fin février), à l'époque de la Semana Santa (Pâques) et à l'occasion des fêtes nationales de la mi-septembre.

Les bus ordinaires sont assez confortables mais, pour les trajets plus longs, les bus avec couchettes (*salón cama*) offrent davantage de place pour étendre les jambes ainsi que des sièges inclinables avec repose-pieds ; leurs tarifs sont supérieurs d'environ 50% à ceux des autres bus. Il est interdit de fumer à bord de tous les bus du pays.

Les bus qui circulent sur les routes secondaires sont plus anciens, plus rudimentaires et moins fréquents (voire inexistants dans les régions les plus isolées). Ces *micros*, qui ne disposent pas toujours de sièges inclinables, sont souvent pris d'assaut par les paysans transportant leurs productions.

Train

Le réseau ferroviaire pour passagers est très limité. Les seules grandes lignes relient la Estación Central de Santiago à Chillán, Concepción, Temuco et les villes intermédiaires au sud (en été jusqu'à Puerto Varas). De petits trains circulent très irrégulièrement de Talca à Constitución, et des lignes de banlieue relient Santiago à Rancagua vers le sud et

Valpa-raíso/Viña del Mar à Villa Alemana et Limache vers l'est.

Les trains des grandes lignes disposent de trois classes : *económica*, *salón* et *dormitorio* (couchettes). La classe couchettes se divise en *cama alta* (couchette supérieure), et *cama baja* (couchette inférieure) plus chère. Sur le trajet de 20 heures entre Santiago et Puerto Varas – le plus long du pays – les billets coûtent environ 105 FF en classe económica, 175 FF en classe salón, 220 FF en cama alta, et 300 FF en cama baja.

Route

Le Chili dispose d'un important réseau de transports publics, mais bon nombre des sites les plus intéressants du pays ne sont accessibles qu'en voiture. Les principales routes nord-sud sont généralement goudronnées et en bon état, à l'exception du célèbre Camino Austral, au sud de Puerto Montt. En revanche, la plupart des routes qui mènent aux

contreforts des Andes et à la cordillère sont de simples pistes de gravier ou de terre battue. Certaines sont en excellent état, tandis que d'autres sont très détériorées ; avant de vous lancer dans de longues excursions dans des régions comme le nord de l'altiplano, renseignez-vous sur l'état des routes et demandez si les pluies récentes n'ont pas rendu certaines régions inaccessibles. Dans certains cas, en l'absence de ponts, il faut recourir à des véhicules spéciaux, de même qu'une voiture 4X4 s'impose parfois pour négocier les passages très boueux.

La location de voiture devient de plus en plus chère, dépassant parfois 500 FF par jour pour les camionettes japonaises *doble cabina* (deux places) à deux roues motrices seulement. Les locations prolongées, d'une semaine ou davantage, peuvent s'avérer assez économiques si l'on voyage en petit groupe. Les voitures

HELEN HUGHES

Local farmer and his ox cart, near Llico, on the west coast of Curico

d'occasion sont si nombreuses au Chili que l'achat d'une voiture constitue, malgré des prix élevés, une solution de plus en plus attrayante pour les visiteurs.

L'utilisation d'une voiture sur place est nettement meilleur marché qu'en Europe : la *bencina* (essence) coûte environ 3 FF le litre, le gasoil étant encore moins cher. Si vous vous éloignez des routes principales, emportez des réserves de carburant.

Le conducteur d'un véhicule doit être muni de tous les papiers d'usage : carte grise, attestation d'assurances et permis de conduire international (à se procurer auprès de votre préfecture).

Bicyclette

Le cyclotourisme constitue aujourd'hui un moyen de plus en plus populaire de découvrir le Chili, en particulier dans la région des lacs et le long du Camino Austral. Toutefois, dans la mesure où seules les artères principales sont goudronnées, et où même les grandes routes sont bordées de bas-côtés très étroits et non goudronnés, la plupart des cyclistes préfèrent recourir au VTT. On peut louer des vélos à des prix raisonnables dans les régions très touristiques, et il est facile de faire réparer les bicyclettes, même si les installations sont parfois limitées dans les lieux les plus isolés.

Bateau

Dans la région des archipels, au sud de Puerto Montt, les services de ferries sont fréquents. L'une des excursions les plus attrayantes et les plus prisées du pays est la croisière de quatre jours et trois nuits reliant Puerto Montt à Puerto Natales. Le circuit en ferry entre Puerto Montt ou Puerto Chacabuco et le Parque Nacional Laguna San Rafael et l'association croisière-excursion en bus avec traversée

du Lago Todos los Santos jusqu'à Bariloche, en Argentine, constituent également de grandes attractions. Les services de ferries plus courts, notamment dans la région de l'Isla Grande de Chiloé, restent avant tout des moyens de transport, mais n'en sont pas moins très agréables.

A l'exception du ferry pour passagers qui relie Punta Arenas à Porvenir, seuls des paquebots de luxe effectuent des croisières sur les itinéraires les plus méridionaux, le long de l'Estrecho de Magallanes (détroit de Magellan).

Île de Pâques

Il n'existe pas de transport public sur Rapa Nui, mais il est pos-sible de louer des VTT, des voitures, des motos et même des chevaux. La randonnée à pied n'est conseillée qu'autour de Hanga Roa en raison de la rareté de l'eau sur le reste de l'île.

Les périodes de location, quel que soit le moyen de transport, sont en général d'une journée, voire de deux jours. Comptez environ 13 $US pour un VTT, 15 $US pour un cheval, 35 $US pour une voiture ordinaire et 50 $US pour un véhicule 4x4. En dehors de la bonne route principale qui devrait bientôt être goudron-née, certaines zones seront mieux practicables avec un 4x4.

HELEN HUGHES

Chilotes, making apple cider with a wooden apple press

Reisen in Chile und auf der Oster Insel

Bus

Chilenische Langstreckenbusse sind schnell, modern, bequem und preiswert. Eine der längsten Fahrten im Land, die Strecke von Arica nach Santiago kostet, für rund 2050 km, in der Sommerhauptsaison US$50. Fahrpreise sind von Unternehmen zu Unternehmen verschieden und Spezialangebote (*ofertas*) können manchmal um die Hälfte billiger sein. Platzreservierungen sind im allgemeinen nicht notwendig, aber in der Sommerhauptsaison (von Weihnachten bis Ende Februar), um Semana Santa (Ostern) und um die patriotischen Feiertage im September herum eine gute Idee.

Gewöhnliche Busse sind relativ bequem, doch für längere Strecken empfiehlt sich ein Schlafbus (*salón cama*), der etwas mehr Beinfreiheit und Liegesitze mit Waden- und Fußstütze bietet. Der Fahrpreis liegt etwa 50% höher als bei anderen Busdiensten. Das Rauchen ist im ganzen Land in allen Bussen verboten.

Auf den Nebenrouten sind die Busse älter, einfacher und seltener (oder an entlegenen Stellen manchmal überhaupt nicht vorhanden). Diese *micros*, welchen es manchmal an Liegesitzen fehlt, können mit Einheimischen und ihren landwirtschaftlichen Produkten vollgestopft sein.

Zug

Passagierbahnverbindungen gibt es nur sehr wenige. Die einzigen Langstreckenverbindungen sind jene von Santiago Estación Central Süd nach Chillán, Concepción, Temuco und den dazwischenliegenden Orten (nur im Sommer gibt es noch eine zusätzliche Verbindung nach Puerto Varas). Vereinzelt gibt es Schmalspurbahnverbindungen von Talca nach Constitución und Pendlerzüge fahren von Santiago Süd nach Rancagua und von Valparaíso/Viño del Mar Ost nach Villa Alemana und Limache.

Langstreckenzüge haben drei Klassen: *económica, salón* und *dormitorio* (Schlafwagen). Die Schlafwagenklasse ist in *cama alta* (oberes Bett) und die teurere *cama baja* (unteres Bett) unterteilt. Auf dem 20-Stunden-Trip von Santiago nach Puerto Varas, die längste Strecke im Land, liegt der Fahrpreis bei ungefähr US$21 für económica, US$35 für salón, US$44 für cama alta und US$60 für cama baja.

Straße

Chiles öffentliches Transportmittelnetz ist ausgedehnt, aber viele der interessantesten Merkmale des Landes können nur mit einem Kraftfahrzeug erreicht werden. Die wichtigsten Nord-Süd-Verbindungsstraßen sind im allgemeinen befestigt und in gutem Zustand, mit Ausnahme des berühmten Camino Austral südlich von Puerto Montt. Doch die meisten Straßen, die in die Ausläufer der Anden und in das Kettengebirge (Cordillera) führen haben entweder nur Kiesbelag oder sind unbefestigt. Manche dieser Straßen sind in ausgezeichnetem, manch

HELEN HUGHES

Smouldering geysers at El Tatio, near the Bolivian border

andere in sehr schlechtem Zustand. Bevor Sie ausgedehnte Ausflüge in Gegenden wie zum Beispiel dem nördlichen Altiplano machen wollen, sollten Sie versuchen den Zustand der Straßen zu eruieren und herauszufinden, ob etwaige Regenfälle manche Streckenabschnitte womöglich unpassierbar gemacht haben. Es kann vorkommen, daß Brücken einfach nicht vorhanden sind und dadurch Flußdurchfahrten notwendig werden; ein Vierradantrieb kann möglicherweise beim Durchqueren von schlammigen Stellen notwendig sein.

Das Mieten eines Autos ist in Chile mittlerweile sehr teuer geworden. Man zahlt pro Tag von US$100 aufwärts für den beliebten *doble cabina* (Zweisitzer) japanischen "Pick-up Truck" (Kleinlastwagen) ohne Vierradantrieb. Eine längere Mietdauer von einer Woche oder mehr, kann für Gruppen relativ preiswert sein. Chiles Vorrat an Gebrauchtwagen macht den Autokauf zu einer sehr attraktiven Möglichkeit. Im Vergleich zu Europa und Nordamerika sind die Autopreise aber immer noch hoch.

Autofahren ist in Chile wesentlich billiger als in Europa, doch teurer als in Nordamerika. Der Preis für *bencina* (Benzin) liegt bei ungefähr US$0.55 pro Liter, doch *gas-oil* (Diesel) ist deutlich billiger. Abseits von befestigten Straßen sollte Sie immer zusätzlichen Treibstoff mitführen.

Ganz gleich welches Fahrzeug Sie fahren, Sie sollten immer alle wichtigen Dokumente, einschließlich Besitznachweis, Versicherung und internationalen Führerschein (bei Autmobilklubs in Ihrem eigenen Land erhätlich), bei sich tragen.

Fahrrad

Fahrradtouren sind eine zunehmend beliebte Art des Reisens in Chile, vor allem in der südlichen Seenregion und entlang dem Camino Austral. Da nur die wichtigsten Nord-Süd-Verbindungsstraßen befestigt sind, wobei sogar diese oft nur schmale, unbefestigte Seitenstreifen haben, ziehen viele Langstreckenradfahrer Mountainbikes vor. Fahrräder können in Touristenzentren ohne große Schwierigkeit zu vernünftigen Preisen gemietet werden. Reparaturstätten für Fahrräder findet man relativ häufig, obwohl an manchen abgelegen Orten Ersatzteile rar sein können.

Boot

Im südlichen archipelischen Chile, südlich von Puerto Montt, gibt es ein großes Angebot an Fähren, die reizvolle Ausfahrten anbieten. Einer der beliebtesten und verlockendsten Trips des Landes ist die vier Tage und drei Nächte dauernde Kreuzfahrt von Puerto Montt nach Puerto Natales. Die Fährenkreuzfahrt von Puerto Montt oder Puerto Chacabuco nach Parque Nacional Laguna San Rafael sowie die Verbindung von Boot und Bus bei einem Ausflug über den Lago Todos Los Santos nach Bariloche in Argentinen, gehören ebenfalls zu den Hauptattraktionen. Kürzere Fährendienste, wie jener in und um Isla Grande de Chiloé, dienen in erster Linie Transportzwecken, doch können trotzdem unterhaltsam sein.

Mit Ausnahme der Passagierfähre von Punta Arenas nach Porvenir befahren ausschließlich Luxuskreuzer die südlichsten Routen entlang der Estrecho de Magallanes (Magellanstraße).

Oster Insel

Offizielle öffentliche Verkehrsmittel gibt es auf Rapa Nui nicht, aber vernünftige Alternativen: Wandern oder das Mieten von Pferden, Mountainbikes, Motrrädern und Autos. Wegen der Wasserknappheit ist Wandern allerdings nur in der Umgebung von Hanga Roa ratsam.

Die normale Mietzeit für alle Transportmittel beträgt 8 Stunden pro Tag. Es ist jedoch möglich, Übernacht-Mieten zu vereinbaren. Der übliche Mietpreis für Mountainbikes beträgt US$13, für Pferde US$15, für ein normales Auto US$35 und für ein Allradfahrzeug US$50. In einigen Gebieten abseits der Hauptinsel Rundstrecke, welche in sehr gutem Zustand ist und bald gepflastert sein könnte, ist es einfacher mit einem Allradfahrzeug.

WAYNE BERNHARDSON

Belltower in the village of
Caquena, Parque Nacional Lauca

Cómo Movilizarse dentro de Chile e Isla de Pascua

En Autobús

Los autobuses a larga distancia de Chile son rápidos, modernos, cómodos y a precios razonables - uno de los viajes más largos dentro del país, desde Arica hasta Santiago que cubre 2.050 kilómetros, cuesta aproximadamente 50 dólares americanos durante el período caro de verano. El costo varía entre las diferentes empresas y las *"ofertas"* pueden reducir el costo de los boletos normales hasta en un 50%. Por lo general no es necesario hacer reservaciones, pero es buena idea hacerlas durante el período de alta demanda del verano (desde la Navidad hasta finales de febrero), alrededor de la Semana Santa, y alrededor de las vacaciones patrióticas a mediados de septiembre.

Los autobuses ordinarios son lo suficiente cómodos, pero en los viajes más largos, los autobuses dormitorio, *"salón de cama"*, ofrecen espacio adicional para las piernas y asientos reclinables con descansadero para las piernas y los pies. El precio de los boletos es aproximadamente 50% más elevado que el de los otros servicios. Está prohibido fumar en todos los autobuses del país.

En Tren

Los servicios ferroviarios de pasajeros son muy limitados. Las únicas rutas a larga distancia van en dirección sur de la Estación Central de Santiago a Chillán, Concepción, Temuco y las poblaciones intermedias (continúa a Puerto Varas pero sólo en verano). Hay una ramificación esporádica de línea ferroviaria de vía estrecha que va de Talca a Constitución, y líneas de pasajeros que van de Santiago hacia el sur a Rancagua y de Valparaíso y Viña del Mar hacia el este a Villa Alemana y Limache.

WAYNE BERNHARDSON

Ceiling mural by Xavier Guerrero, Escuela Mexico, Chillán

Los trenes de rutas a larga distancia tienen tres clases: económica, *salón* y *dormitorio*. La clase dormitorio está dividida en *cama alta* y la más cara, *cama baja*. Para el viaje de 20 horas de Santiago a Puerto Varas, el viaje más largo del país, los boletos valen aproximadamente $US21 en clase económica, $US35 en salón, $US44 en cama alta y $US60 en cama baja.

Por Carretera

La red de transporte público de Chile es extensa, pero muchos de los aspectos más interesantes de Chile se pueden apreciar sólo en vehículo automotor. Las autopistas principales que van de norte a sur generalmente están pavimentadas y en buenas condiciones, a excepción del famoso Camino Austral al sur de Puerto Montt. Pero la mayoría de las carreteras que van hacia el pie de las colinas y a la cordillera de los Andes están cubiertas de cascajo o están sin asfaltar. Algunas de éstas son excelentes pero algunas otras están en muy malas condiciones. Antes de iniciar excursiones extensas a zonas como el norte del altiplano, se debe tratar de verificar las condiciones de las carreteras y averiguar si las lluvias recientes han hecho que algunas de estas zonas sean impasables. Puede que los puentes no existan, lo que haría necesario ir vadeando y el uso de vehículos de tracción en las cuatro ruedas para pasar las zonas de lodo.

El costo del alquiler de vehículos a ido cada vez más en

aumento y, a menudo, es mas de los $US100 al día por las populares camionetas japonesas de *doble cabina* sin tracción en las cuatro ruedas. El alquiler por períodos largos, de una semana o más, puede resultar relativamente económico para grupos. La disponibilidad de vehículos de segunda mano en Chile ha hecho que la compra de un vehículo sea una opción cada vez más atractiva para los visitantes, pero, aun así, los precios son más altos de los correspondientes en Europa y Norte América.

La operación de un vehículo en Chile es más barata que en Europa pero más cara que en Norte América. El precio de la *bencina* es de aproximadamente $US0.55 por litro. El precio del *diesel* es significativamente más bajo. Se deben llevar reservas de combustible si se va a salir de las autopistas principales.

Los conductores de cualquier vehículo deben llevar todos los documentos necesarios, inclusive la prueba de propiedad, el seguro y la Licencia Internacional de Conducir (que se puede obtener en el club de automotores de su propio país).

En Bicicleta

El viaje en bicicleta se ha convertido en una forma cada vez más popular de recorrer Chile, especialmente en la región sur de los lagos y a lo largo del Camino Austral. Debido a que solamente las autopistas longitudinales principales están pavimentadas e inclusive éstas a menudo tienen hombros estrechos sin pavimentar, la mayoría de los ciclistas de larga distancia prefieren bicicletas de montaña. Las bicicletas de alquiler son fáciles de obtener a precios razonables en las zonas de gran turismo, y los lugares de reparaciones son comunes, aunque en lugares aislados los repuestos pueden ser muy escasos.

En Bote

En la zona sur de los archipiélagos de Chile, desde Puerto Montt hacia el sur, son comunes los servicios turísticos de viajes en bote. Uno de los viajes más populares y que más gusta es el crucero de cuatro días y tres noches desde Puerto Montt hasta Puerto Natales. También son atracciones de gran importancia el crucero que va desde Puerto Montt o desde Puerto Chacabuco al Parque Nacional Laguna San Rafael y la excursión combinada de bote y autobús por el Lago Todos los Santos hasta Bariloche, Argentina. Los servicios de viajes en bote más cortos, como los que se ofrecen en y alrededor de Isla Grande de Chiloé tienen como objetivo primordial el transporte, pero también son muy agradables.

A excepción del bote de pasajeros que va de Punta Arenas a Porvenir, solamente los cruceros de lujo se aventuran a las rutas que van más hacia el sur a lo largo del Estrecho de Magallanes.

Isla de Pascua

En Rapa Nui no hay ningún transporte organizado, pero movilizarse a pie, a caballo, con bicicleta de montaña, con motocicleta o en coche son opciones razonables. Debido a la escasez de agua, la movilización a pie sólo se recomienda para los lugares cercanos a Hanga Roa.

El tiempo de alquiler para todas los medios de transporte es de una jornada de 8 horas, aunque es posible hacer arreglos para alquilar durante la noche. Los precios promedio de alquiler son $US13,00 por una bicicleta de montaña, $US15,00 por un caballo, $US35,00 por un coche de pasajeros normal y $US50,00 por un vehiculo de tracción a cuatro ruedas. En algunas zonas que no forman parte del circuito principal, el cual es muy bueno y pronto estará pavimentado, es mejor utilizar un vehículo de tracción a cuatro ruedas.

WAYNE BERNHARDSON

Mural of Fiesta de la Virgen del Carmen at La Tirana, Tarapacá

チリとイースター島の旅

バス

チリの長距離バスは、スピードが速く近代的な設備も整っていて乗り心地がよく値段も比較的安い。国内の最長距離路線のひとつ、アリカ(Arica)、サンティアゴ(Santiago)間の2050kmは夏のピークシーズンでもUS$50程度だ。料金は会社によって異なるが、特別割引の場合(オフェルタス: *ofertas*)、普通料金の半額まで下がることもある。予約は通常必要ないが、夏のピーク

シーズン(クリスマスから2月の終わりまで)、復活祭(セマナ・サンタ: Semana Santa)、9月末の愛国記念日は予約を勧める。

普通のバスも乗り心地は十分にいいが、長距離旅行には足を伸ばせるスペースと、足置き付きのリクライニングシートが設備された寝台バス(サロン・カマ: *sal cama*)がある。料金はほかのバスよりも50%ほど割高。国内路線は全て車内禁煙だ。

2級路線のバスは古く、設備があまり整っていず、本数も少ない(遠隔地域には路線がないところもある)。このようなバス(ミクロス: *micros*)はリクライニングシートがないこと、現地の人や農産物でいっぱいのことが時々ある。

電車

旅客列車の本数は大変限られている。唯一の長距離路線はサンティアゴのエスタシオン・セントラル(Estaci Central)から、南部のチヤン(Chill疣)、コンセプシオン (Concepci)、テムコ(Temuco)、そして中部(夏期のみプエルト・バラス: Puerto Varasまで接続)までの路線だけだ。不定期的でゲージが狭いタルカ(Talca)からコンスティトゥシオン(Constituci)までの支線、サンティアゴから南のランカグア(Rancagua)までの通勤線、バルバライソ/ビニャ・デル・マル(Valpara o/Vi del Mar)から東のビヤ・アレマナ(Villa Alemana) とリマチェ(Limache)までの通勤線がある。

長距離線の客車は3つのクラスがある。エコノミカ(*econ ica*)、サロン(*sal*)、そして、寝台車(ドルミトリオ: *dormitorio*)だ。寝台車のクラスはさらに上部の寝台(カマ・アルタ: *cama alta*)と多少料金が高めの下部の寝台(カマ・バジャ: *cama baja*)に別れている。国内で最も長いサンティアゴからプエルト・ヴァラスまでの20時間の旅はエコノミカで約US$21、サロンで約US$35、カマ・アルタでUS$44、カマ・バジャでUS$60。

WAYNE BERNHARDSON

Moai at Rano Raraku, Easter Island

道路

チリの公共輸送機関は広い範囲に行き渡っているが、最も素晴らしい見所は自動車でしかアクセスできないことが多い。有名なカミノ・アウストラル(Camino Austral)から南のプエルト・モント(Puerto Montt)までの部分を除けば、南北に通っているハイウェイはだいたい舗装されていて、いいコンディションのものが多いが、アンデスの丘陵地帯および山系に入る道は砂利または未舗装だ。このうちのいくつかはとてもよく整備されているが、その他の道はコンディションがとても悪い。北部高原地帯などに入るときは、最近の雨で通行不可能になっているかどうか、あらかじめ道の状態を調べておくこと。橋がかかっていなかったために浅瀬を渡らなくてはいけなかったり、泥道と格闘するために4WDが必要だったりすることもある。

レンタカーは最近高くなってきている。例えば、人気が高い荷台付き日本車(ドブル・カビナ：doble cabina)は、4WDではないが、一日だいたいUS$100から。1週間以上の長期の場合はグループで借りると経済的。チリで中古車を購入する旅行客が増えてきたが、ヨーロッパや北アメリカに比べると高めだ。

チリの燃料費はヨーロッパに比べるとずっと安いが、北アメリカに比べると高い。ガソリン(ベンシナ：bencina)は1リットルUS$0.55だが、ディーゼル(ガスオイル：gas-oil)は大変安い。主要舗装道から離れるときは予備の燃料を持っていくこと。

運転手は車の所有証明書、保険、国際免許証(自国の自動車協会で申請する)などの書類を必ず所持していること。

自転車

自転車ツアーはチリ国内、特に南部の湖沼地域とカミノ・アウストラル沿いを旅行する手段として最近人気が出てきた。舗装道は南北に通る主要国道だけ、その上このような道路も路肩が狭く舗装していないところが多いので、長距離のサイクリング・ツアーにはマウンテン・バイクが好まれる。貸自転車はサイクリングがよく行われる地域では安い値段で借りることができ、修理のための施設も多い。しかし、遠隔地域では部品の入手は難しいことがある。

ボート

プエルト・モントから南のチリ南部の群島地帯では観光フェリーが多い。この国で最も魅力的で人気が高い旅のひとつはプエルト・モントからプエルト・ナタレス(Puerto Natales)までの3泊4日のクルーズだ。プエルト・モントまたはプエルト・チャカブコ(Puerto Chacabuco)からサン・ラファエル・ラグーン国立公園(Parque Nacional Laguna San Rafael)までのフェリーのクルージング、そしてラゴ・トドス(Lago Todos)、ロス・サントス(Los Santos)から、バリョチェ(Bariloche)、アルゼンチンまでのバスとボートを組み合わせたツアーも見所。大チロエ島(Isla Grande de Chiloé)付近をめぐる短距離フェリーはごく普通の乗客輸送用だが、とても楽しいもののひとつだ。

マゼラン海峡(エストレチョ・デ・マガヤネス：Estrecho de Magallanes)を往来するのは、プンタ・アレナス(Punta Arenas)からポルベニル(Porvenir)までの乗客フェリーの他に、高級クルーズだけしかない。

イースター島

ラパ・ニュイ(Rapa Nui)には公共交通機関がないが、徒歩、乗馬、マウンテンバイク、オートバイ、自動車という選択がある。徒歩は水が手に入らないので、ハンガ・ロア(Hanga Roa)近辺のみ推薦する。どんな交通手段も基本レンタル時間は8時間だが、翌日まで借りることも可能。

典型的なレンタル費用は、マウンテンバイクがUS13ドル、乗馬がUS15ドル、乗用車がUS35ドル、四駆がUS50ドル。一番大きい島の環状道路は状態が良く、近々舗装される予定だが、この道路から離れる時は四駆のほうが良い。

WAYNE BERNHARDSON

Torre Reloj, Pisagua

Index

Note: Geographical and cultural features are also listed separately at the end of the general index in their appropriate categories.

GENERAL INDEX
All listed placenames are in Chile except:

A - Argentina
B - Bolivia
El - Easter Island
P - Peru

For duplicate names in Chile the province abbreviations are:

Ais - Aisén
Ant - Antofagasta
Ara - La Araucanía
Ata - Atacama
Bio - Biobío
Coq - Coquimbo
JF - Juan Fernandez
Lag - Los Lagos
Mag - Magallanes
Mau - Maule
Ohi - O'Higgins
San - Santiago
Tar - Tarapacá
Val - Valparaíso

Abtao 36 D4
Achacaltambo 11 E3
Achao 36 D5
Acoribea (B) 11 F5
Adolfo Zaldivar 17 G4
Aduana Pejerrey 31 E5
Afquintué 34 D3
Agua Buena 16 D5
Agua Fresca 52 A2
Agua Grande 25 E3
Agua Helada 21 E5
Aguantao 36 D4
Agua Santa 32 D6
Aguas Blancas (Ant) 17 E4
Aguas Blancas (Ant) 18 B2
Aguas Buenas 36 C4
Aguas Calientes 37 F1
Aguas de la Gloria 32 C1
Agua Verde 20 D2
Ahoni 36 D6
Ahu Tepeu 19 (El) F2
Ahu Tongariki (El)19 G2
Ahu Vinapu (El) 19 F3
Aiquina 15 G5
Aitui 36 D6
Alcohuas 25 F5
Alcones 28 C6
Alcorta 14 C6
Alerce 37 E3
Alfalfal 29 G3
Algarrobal 22 C5
Algarrobito 24 D4
Algarrobo 28 D3
Alicahue 27 E5
Allipén 34 D2
Almagro 34 D1
Almendrillo 27 F5
Almirante Latorre 25 E3
Altamira 20 D3
Alto Butalcura 36 C5
Alto Caledonia 33 E4
Alto Colorado 28 C5

Alto del Carmen 22 C6
Alto Hospicio 12 B4
Alto Jahuel 29 F4
Alto Nahuelbuta 32 B4
Alto Retamilla 12 C2
Alto Río Mayo (A) 41 H2
Altos de Pica 13 E5
Altos de Talinay 24 C6
Altovalsol 24 D4
Altuza 12 D1
Aluminé (A) 35 H3
Amargos 34 B4
Amincha 15 G1
Amolanas 22 D4
Anakena (El) 19 G1
Ancagual 34 D3
Ancopujo 10 D3
Ancud 36 C4
Andachildo 36 D6
Andacollo 25 E5
Andacollo (A) 33 H2
Angol 32 C4
Angostura (Coq) 26 C3
Angostura (Ohi) 29 E6
Anticura 35 H3
Antiguala 32 B4
Antilhué 34 C4
Antillanca 37 F1
Antofagasta 16 C3
Antonia 52 C2
Antuco 33 F3
Apiao 36 D6
Arauco 32 B3
Arbolillo 30 C4
Archipiélago de las Guaitecas 38 C4
Archipiélago de los Chonos 38 A6-B5
Archipiélago Guayaneco 42 B2
Archipiélago Reina Adelaida 46 D5
Área de Protección Radal Siete Tazas 31 F3
Arenal 30 C4
Arepunta 10 D6
Arica 10 B5
Ariquilda 12 D3
Armerillo 31 F4
Arquilhue 35 E5
Arrequintín (A) 25 H5
Arroyo Potrerillo (A) 27 H3
Artificio 29 E1
Ascotán 15 G3
Astillas 22 B5
Astillero 31 E3
Aucanquilcha 15 G1
Aucar 36 D5
Auchemo 39 E1
Auco 26 D3
Augusta Victoria 17 F4
Aulén 37 E4
Aurora 30 D3
Ausipar 10 C5
Ayacara 37 E5
Azapa 10 B5
Azufrera 21 G3

Bahía Adventure 38 B6
Bahía Agua Fresca 52 A2
Bahía Anna Pink 40 B3
Bahía Asasao 38 C2
Bahía Barrister 50 C1
Bahía Beaufort 47 E6
Bahía Bossi 44 B3
Bahía Breaker 51 E3
Bahía Brookes 52 C5

Bahía Carrizal 24 C2
Bahía Chanco 30 B4
Bahía Chiquinata 12 B4
Bahía Chomache 14 B1
Bahía Choros 24 D2
Bahía Cobquecura 30 B5
Bahía Cocotué 36 C4
Bahía Coliumo 30 A6
Bahía Conchali 26 C4
Bahía Cook 54 B1
Bahía Copiapó 22 B2
Bahía Coquimbo 24 D4
Bahía Cucao 36 B6
Bahía Cumberland (JF) 19 H5
Bahía Darwin 40 B2
Bahía de Caldera 22 B1
Bahía de Carnero 32 A3
Bahía de la Colonia (JF) 19 E6
Bahía de La Perouse (El) 19 G1
Bahía de Laguna Verde 28 D2
Bahía del Sur 55 E3
Bahía de Mejillones del Sur 16 C1
Bahía de San Pedro 36 C1
Bahía Dineley 42 A6
Bahía Expectación 44 C4
Bahía Felipe 48 C6
Bahía Filton 52 B5
Bahía Gallegos (A) 49 E2
Bahía Gente Grande 48 C6
Bahía Guanaqueros 24 D5
Bahía Harvey 42 B2
Bahía Herradura de Guayacán 24 D4
Bahía Ibáñez 41 G4
Bahía Inglesa (Ata) 22 B2
Bahía Inglesa 22 B1
Bahía Inútil 52 C2
Bahía Isla Blanca 20 B2
Bahía Jara 41 G4
Bahía Las Cañas 30 B3
Bahía La Vaquería (JF) 19 H5
Bahía Lee 48 C6
Bahía Linao 36 D4
Bahía Lomas 49 E5
Bahía Maiquillahue 34 C3
Bahía Manao 36 D4
Bahía Manea 34 B6
Bahía Maullín 36 C3
Bahía Moreno 16 C2
Bahía Nassau 55 F2
Bahía Nuestra Señora 20 C2
Bahía Oglander 55 H2
Bahía Otway 50 D2
Bahía Parker 46 D5
Bahía Porvenir 52 B2
Bahía Posesión 49 E4
Bahía Queule 34 C3
Bahía Salado 22 B3
Bahía Salvación 44 B6
Bahía San Andrés 40 A5
Bahía San Francisco 55 G4
Bahía San Quintín 40 C5
Bahía San Sebastián (A) 53 E1
Bahía Santiago 48 D5
Bahía Spartan 44 A3
Bahía Stewart (Ais) 40 A4
Bahía Stewart (Mag) 51 H6
Bahía Stokes 51 F4
Bahía Tarn 42 C2
Bahía Teniente 26 C1
Bahía Tic Toc 39 E3
Bahía Tierras Blancas (JF) 19 G5
Bahía Tongoy 24 C5
Bahía Totoralillo 20 B6

Bahía Tribune 42 C5
Bahía Whitesand 48 B6
Bahía Windhond 55 F2
Bahía Wodsworth 47 E6
Bajos de San Agustín 29 F3
Balada 25 F4
Balmaceda (Ant) 20 D1
Balmaceda (Ais) 41 H3
Balneario Flamenco 20 B6
Balneario Obispito 20 B6
Balneario Portofino 20 B5
Baño Nuevo 41 H1
Baños Campanario 31 G4
Baños de Chihuio 35 E5
Baños de Colina 29 H4
Baños del Toro 25 G4
Baños de Turi 15 G4
Baños Morales 29 G4
Baquedano (Ant) 17 E2
Bardas Blancas (A) 31 H4
Barquito 20 B5
Barrancas (A) 39 H2
Barranquillas 22 B3
Barraza 24 D6
Barreal (A) 27 H3
Barriles 14 B4
Barros Arana 34 D2
Barros Luco 22 C3
Batuco 30 C3
Belco 30 C4
Belén 10 D5
Bellavista (Lag) 34 C6
Bellavista (Ais) 41 H2
Bellavista (A) 33 H2
Bilbao 32 D6
Blanco Encalada 16 C5
Boca 29 E1
Boca Budi 34 C1
Boca de Canales 42 C2
Boca del Guafo 38 B3
Bolaco 20 C3
Bollenar 29 E3
Boroa 34 D1
Botalcura 30 D3
Brazo Chacabuco 43 G6
Brazo Noreste 43 G5
Brazo Noroeste 43 F5
Brazo Norte (A) 45 F4
Brazo Oeste 43 F5
Brazo Sur (A) 45 F5
Brazo Sur del Río Coig (A) 48 A2
Breas 20 C3
Bucalemu (Val) 28 D4
Bucalemu (Ohi) 28 C6
Buchupureo 30 B5
Buena Esperanza 22 B6
Buenos Aires Chico (A) 37 H4
Buenuraqui 32 C2
Buill 37 E5
Buin 29 F4
Bulnes 32 D1

Caba de Lata (A) 35 G5
Cabeceras 28 C6
Cabeza del Mar 48 B6
Cabildo 27 E6
Cabo Bascuñán 24 C1
Cabo Condell 10 B5
Cabo Cumming (El) 19 H2
Cabo de Hornos 55 G4
Cabo Domingo (A) 53 F3
Cabo Espíritu Santo (A) 49 F6
Cabo Expectación 52 C4
Cabo Froward 51 H3

Cabo Jara 16 C3
Cabo Leones 24 C1
Cabo Norte (El) 19 F1
Cabo Norte (JF) 19 E6
Cabo O'Higgins (El) 19 H2
Cabo Paquita 14 B3
Cabo Quedal 36 C2
Cabo Roggewein (El) 19 H2
Cabo Rugged 44 B4
Cabo San Isidro 52 A3
Cabo San Pío (A) 55 H1
Cabo San Sebastián (A) 53 F2
Cabo Sur (El) 19 F3
Cabo Vírgenes (A) 49 F5
Cabrero 32 D2
Cachagua 26 D6
Cachapoal 30 D6
Cachiyuyo 25 E1
Cahuil 28 C6
Cahuisa 13 E6
Caimanes 26 D4
Caipé (A) 18 B6
Caipulli 36 C4
Cajón 34 D1
Cajón Troncoso 31 F5
Calabozos 30 C5
Calachuz 15 F3
Calacoto (B) 11 G1
Calafquén (Lag) 35 E3
Calafquén (Lag) 35 E3
Calama 15 E5
Calatambo 12 C2
Calbuco 36 D4
Caldera 22 B1
Calera de Tango 29 F3
Caleta Agua Dulce 16 C4
Caleta Agua Salada 16 C4
Caleta Anakena (El) 19 G1
Caleta Andrade 41 E1
Caleta Apolillado 24 C2
Caleta Arrayán 24 D3
Caleta Ayacara 37 E5
Caleta Bandurria del Sur 16 C2
Caleta Barco 28 D2
Caleta Barquito 20 B5
Caleta Barranquillas 22 B3
Caleta Blanco Encalada 16 C5
Caleta Bolfín 16 C3
Caleta Botija 16 C5
Caleta Boy 14 B4
Caleta Buena 12 B3
Caleta Buena (Ant) 14 B5
Caleta Caramucho 12 B6
Caleta Chacaya 14 B6
Caleta Chaihuin 34 B4
Caleta Chañaral (Ata) 24 D2
Caleta Chañaral 24 C1
Caleta Chica 12 B2
Caleta Chipana 14 B2
Caleta Chucumata 12 B5
Caleta Cifuncho 20 B3
Caleta Colorada 16 C6
Caleta Coloso 16 C3
Caleta Cóndor 36 C1
Caleta de Camarones 12 B1
Caleta de Gatico 14 B5
Caleta del Medio 22 B3
Caleta El Cobre (Ant) 16 C5
Caleta El Cobre 16 C5
Caleta El Pedregal 20 B5
Caleta Esmeralda 20 B4
Caleta Esperanza 52 C2
Caleta Flamenco 20 B6
Caleta Gonzalo 37 E6
Caleta Gualagula 14 B6
Caleta Gualaihue 37 E4
Caleta Guanillo del Norte 14 B2
Caleta Guanillo del Sur 14 B5

Caleta Guayasca 36 C1
Caleta Herradura de Mejillones 16 C1
Caleta Hanga Oteo (El) 19 F1
Caleta Horcón 26 D6
Caleta Hotuiti (El) 19 G2
Caleta Junín 12 B2
Caleta La Arena 37 E3
Caleta Lacao 26 C2
Caleta La Ligua 26 D5
Caleta Lameguapi 34 B5
Caleta Las Docas 28 D2
Caleta La Serena 30 B4
Caleta Lautaro 14 B2
Caleta Loa 14 B2
Caleta Los Hornos 24 D3
Caleta Maicolpué 34 B6
Caleta Maitencillo de Coquimbo
    26 C2
Caleta Mala 26 C3
Caleta Mansa 34 B6
Caleta Mataura 46 C6
Caleta Mejillones del Norte 12 B3
Caleta Michilla 14 B6
Caleta Milagro 34 B5
Caleta Molles 26 D5
Caleta Morritos 26 C2
Caleta Morritos Norte 26 C2
Caleta Navidad 28 C4
Caleta Obispito 20 B6
Caleta Obispo 20 B6
Caleta Oscuro 26 C3
Caleta Pabellón de Pica 12 B6
Caleta Pajonal 22 B3
Caleta Pan de Azúcar (Ata) 20 B4
Caleta Pan de Azúcar 20 B4
Caleta Pisagua Viejo 12 B2
Caleta Playa Tontado 22 A6
Caleta Puelche 37 E4
Caleta Punta Arenas 14 B3
Caleta Quidico 32 B5
Caleta Río Seco 14 B1
Caleta Santa Bárbara 37 E6
Caleta Sarco 22 A6
Caleta Tames 14 B6
Caleta Tirúa 32 B6
Caleta Tortel 43 E3
Caleta Totoral Bajo 22 A4
Caleta Totoral de Lengua de Vaca
    24 C5
Caleta Totoralillo 24 D3
Caleta Tragagente 16 C5
Caleta Tumán 28 C5
Caleta Vítor 10 B5
Caleta Zenteno 20 B6
Caletones 29 F5
Calientes (P) 10 B3
Calingasta (A) 27 H3
Callapa (B) 11 H1
Callaqui 33 F4
Calle Larga 29 F1
Camapento Ancoa 31 E4
Camar 18 B2
Camarico 31 E2
Camarico Viejo 24 D6
Camerón 52 C3
Camarones (Tar) 10 C6
Camarones (Coq) 27 E4
Camiña 12 D2
Campamento Enaex 15 E5
Campamento Manantiales 48 D5
Campanario 33 E2
Campo de Hielo Norte 40 D6
Campo de Hielo Sur 43 E5, 45 E1
Campo de Piedra Pómez 13 G6
Campos de Hielo de San Valentín
    40 D5
Canal Abra 51 E2
Canal Adalberto 42 C5

Canal Albatros 42 B4
Canal Andrés 44 C4
Canal Apiao 36 D6
Canal Baker 43 E4
Canal Ballenero 52 A6
Canal Bárbara 51 G4
Canal Barbarrosa 42 B3
Canal Beagle 55 G1
Canal Castillo 42 A5
Canal Castro 46 C2
Canal Cheap 40 B6-C6
Canal Cockburn 51 G5
Canal Concepción 44 C5
Canal Costa 40 D2
Canal Cutler 46 D3
Canal Darwin 40 C2
Canal de Chacao 36 C4
Canal de los Témpanos (A) 45 F4
Canal Desertores 37 E6
Canal Errázuriz 40 D2
Canal Esmeralda 46 C5
Canal Esteban 44 C5
Canal Euston 47 G5
Canal Fallos 42 B4
Canal Farquhar 42 D5
Canal Ignacio 44 B6
Canal King 38 C5
Canal Ladrillero 44 B1
Canal Magdalena 52 A4
Canal Mesier 42 C3
Canal Miramar 44 A2
Canal Moraleda 38 D5
Canal Murray 55 E1
Canal Octubre 42 A4
Canal Oeste 44 B5
Canal Picton 44 B2
Canal Pitt 44 D5
Canal Puyuguapi 39 E6
Canal Romanche 55 E3
Canal Sarmiento de Gamboa 46 D2
Canal Smith 46 D3-D6
Canal Trinidad 44 B3
Canal Troya 43 E3
Canal Uribe 46 C3
Canal Valdés 47 F3
Canal Whiteside 52 B3
Canal Wide 44 D3
Cancha Alegre 30 C5
Cancha Carrera (A) 47 G1
Cancosa 13 F3
Cancura 37 E1
Candelaria 32 D3
Canela 27 E3
Canela Alta 26 D3
Canela Baja 26 D3
Cañete 32 B4
Cañicura 33 E3
Cañitas 36 D2
Canteras 33 E3
Canto del Agua 22 B5
Canutillar 37 F3
Capitán Pastene 32 C5
Capote 22 B5
Caquena 11 E4
Caracol 34 C6
Carahue 34 C1
Carampangue 32 B3
Caranguillas (B) 11 F5
Carcote 15 G2
Cardonal 28 C6
Carelmapu 36 C4
Carén (Coq) 27 E1
Carén (Coq) 27 E3
Cariquima 13 F2
Caritaya 10 D6
Carmen Alto 17 E2
Carrenleufú 39 G3
Carrera Pinto 22 D1

Carririñe 35 F4
Carrizal Bajo 22 A4
Carrizalillo 24 D2
Cartagena 28 D3
Cartago 33 E2
Casa Blanca 31 E2
Casablanca 28 D3
Casas de Chacabuco 29 F2
Cascada de los Novios 37 G2
Caserón (Ata) 22 C2
Caserón (A) 22 B2
Caserones 25 E4
Casma 36 D2
Caspana 15 G5
Castaño Nuevo (A) 27 H2
Castaño Viejo (A) 27 H1
Castilla 22 C4
Castro 36 C5
Casuto 26 D4
Catalina (Ant) 20 D2
Catalina 49 F6
Catamutún 34 C5
Catanlil (A) 35 H4
Catapilco 26 D6
Catariri (B) 11 F5
Catemu 29 E1
Catúa (A) 18 D4
Caulín 36 D4
Cauquenes 30 C5
Cavilolén 26 D4
Cayucupil 32 B4
Cayutué 37 F2
Cebollar 15 G2
Centinela 17 F2
Central (Lag) 37 E1
Central (Tar) 10 C4
Central (Tar) 12 C5
Central Los Cipreses 31 F4
Central Los Molles 25 F6
Central Rapel 28 D5
Cerillos (Coq) 24 D4
Cerillos (Val) 27 E6
Cero de la Mica 14 C3
Cerrillo Tana 12 C2
Cerrillos de Tamaya 24 D6
Cerritos Bayos 15 E6
Cerro Aconcagua (A) 27 G6
Cerro Acotango (A) 11 E4
Cerro Agua Amarga 21 G3
Cerro Aguas Blancas 21 H3
Cerro Aguas Calientes 21 G1
Cerro Agudo (JF) 19 H5
Cerro Aguja 54 D1
Cerro Aguja Sur 37 G5
Cerro Alesna 43 F5
Cerro Alto (JF) 19 H5
Cerro Alto (A) 25 G6
Cerro Alto Nevado 39 E6
Cerro Alto Toroni 13 F3
Cerro Amaculla 13 E6
Cerro Anarabe 10 D5
Cerro Aracar (A) 18 B5
Cerro Aralar 15 E5
Cerro Araral (B) 15 G3
Cerro Arenales 40 D6
Cerro Arintica 11 E5
Cerro Arroyo Hondo (A) 31 H4
Cerro Atajaña 12 B2
Cerro Atalaya (Ant) 21 G2
Cerro Atalaya (Mag) 47 F6
Cerro Azufre o Copiapó 23 F2
Cerro Azul 31 F4
Cerro Baker 41 G6
Cerro Balmaceda 47 F2
Cerro Bayo de Chocay (A) 31 H4
Cerro Belén 10 D5
Cerro Bertrand 45 E3
Cerro Birrete 17 E1

Cerro Blanco (San) 29 F2
Cerro Blanco (Ant) 15 F3
Cerro Blanco (Ata) 21 F5
Cerro Blanco (Mag) 45 E6
Cerro Bolados 45 E4
Cerro Bonete 43 E1
Cerro Bonete (A) 23 G4
Cerro Bravo 21 F6
Cerro Bravo (A) 31 H3
Cerro Cáceres 39 G5
Cerro Cachina 20 B4
Cerro Caldera 39 F4
Cerro Camaraca 10 B5
Cerro Campana 41 F3
Cerro Carbiri (B) 11 E3
Cerro Carrizalillo 23 E3
Cerro Casillahui (B) 11 G5
Cerro Castillo 47 G1
Cerro Catedral 40 C6
Cerro Catedral (A) 37 H2
Cerro Centinela 17 G2
Cerro Cerrucho 42 A4
Cerro Ceusis 15 F1
Cerro Chañarcito 20 D5
Cerro Checo 22 D3
Cerro Chela 15 F2
Cerro Chicharras 22 C2
Cerro Chilinchilin 13 E4
Cerro Chiliques 18 B3
Cerro Choquelimpie 10 D4
Cerro Chunchuga 13 E4
Cerro Circular 40 C5
Cerro Coipasa (B) 13 G2
Cerro Colachi 18 C2
Cerro Colonia 43 F1
Cerro Colorado (Ant) 15 F3
Cerro Colorado (Ais) 41 G1
Cerro Colupo 14 C5
Cerro Cónico 39 G2
Cerro Constancia 12 C4
Cerro Coposa 13 F6
Cerro Corcovado 21 E3
Cerro Cosapilla 10 D3
Cerro Cristales 16 C4
Cerro Cristales 25 E2
Cerro Cuche 39 H2
Cerro Cuestecillas 22 B4
Cerro Cumbre Rojiza 41 G5
Cerro Cúpula 43 G3
Cerro Darwin 52 D6
Cerro Daudet 45 F5
Cerro de la Cruz 14 C4
Cerro de la Iglesia 23 E5
Cerro de la Laguna (A) 29 H5
Cerro de la Pena 21 G1
Cerro de La Pólvora 21 E3
Cerro de la Posada 14 C3
Cerro de las Gualtatas 25 E6
Cerro de las Yeguas 31 G3
Cerro de la Torre 37 H2
Cerro del Castaño 23 E3
Cerro del Guanaco 28 D3
Cerro del Medio 21 F2
Cerro del Medio 39 E2
Cerro del Morado 27 F5
Cerro de los Escalones 29 F6
Cerro de los Patitos 21 G3
Cerro del Placetón 22 D6
Cerro del Profeta 17 F6
Cerro del Quimal 17 H1
Cerro del Rincón (A&C) 18 C4
Cerro del Sauce 22 B5
Cerro del Volcán 25 F6
Cerro del Yesillo 29 G4
Cerro de Monardes 23 F2
Cerro de Olivares (A) 25 H5
Cerro de Pili 18 C2
Cerro de Puralaco 34 C3

Cerro Desamparado 14 C2
Cerro Desfiladero 25 G5
Cerro de Soga 12 D2
Cerro Diadema 47 G5
Cerro Divisadero 41 G2
Cerro Donoso 47 F1
Cerro Elena 40 B5
Cerro El Fraile (P) 10 C2
Cerro el Picazo 41 F3
Cerro El Potro 23 E5
Cerro El Toro 22 C6
Cerro El Volcán (B) 11 F5
Cerro Encinas 40 B4
Cerro Ermitaño 21 G6
Cerro Esperanza 43 F4
Cerro Estancilla 23 E4
Cerro Florida 20 C4
Cerro Florido 31 E6
Cerro Fonck 40 C4
Cerro Gordo 12 D6
Cerro Graves 52 B3
Cerro Guachacollo (B) 13 H2
Cerro Higuerita 13 E6
Cerro Hornilla 29 G4
Cerro Hudson 41 F3
Cerro Huemul 45 F2
Cerro Iglesias 41 G3
Cerro Inacaliri o del Cajón 15 H4
Cerro Incacamachi (B) 11 G6
Cerro Indice (A) 45 H3
Cerro Italia 52 D6
Cerro La Bandera 41 H2
Cerro La Chira 16 D5
Cerro la Gloria 41 G2
Cerro La Silueta 47 G4
Cerro La Temera 23 E2
Cerro Laiquina (B) 13 G4
Cerro Las Gualas 31 G3
Cerro Las Tórtolas 25 G4
Cerro Latarana 13 E1
Cerro Lejía 18 B3
Cerro Lirima 13 F3
Cerro Livilcar 10 C5
Cerro Llanquipa 11 E6
Cerro Lliscaya 11 E6
Cerro Los Leones 29 G2
Cerro Macizo 33 F4
Cerro Mancha Larga 39 G5
Cerro Maravilla 31 E6
Cerro Marmolejo 29 H4
Cerro Mayo 52 B5
Cerro Mediterráneo 42 D5
Cerro Mejillones 12 C3
Cerro Mercedario (A) 27 G4
Cerro Middleton 44 C3
Cerro Miscanti 18 B3
Cerro Mocho 43 F5
Cerro Morado 29 G4
Cerro Moreno 12 C3
Cerro Nacimiento (A) 23 H2
Cerro Nahuel Pan (A) 39 H1
Cerro Nahuelbuta 32 C4
Cerro Napa 12 C3
Cerro Negro (Bio) 32 D2
Cerro Negro 33 F2
Cerro Negro (A) 45 F4
Cerro Norte (A) 45 F2
Cerro Obelisco 45 G5
Cerro O'Higgins 43 F5
Cerro Oscuro 40 B4
Cerro Overo (A) 29 G6
Cerro Oyarbide 12 B5
Cerro Pacocagua (B) 11 F6
Cerro Paine Grande 45 F6
Cerro Pajonal (A) 21 H3
Cerro Paloana 15 F2
Cerro Palo Negro 22 B4
Cerro Pan de Azúcar 17 E5

Cerro Paranal 16 C6
Cerro Paroma 13 G6
Cerro Patillos 12 B6
Cerro Peine 43 F5
Cerro Peñafiel 21 E1
Cerro Perales 20 C2
Cerro Piga 13 F4
Cerro Pingo (Ant) 20 C3
Cerro Pingo (Ata) 21 E6
Cerro Pingo Pingo 17 H4
Cerro Pirámide 47 F6
Cerro Piquenes 29 H3
Cerro Plomo (Ant) 17 F4
Cerro Plomo (San) 29 G2
Cerro Pular 18 A5
Cerro Punta Ramada 10 B6
Cerro Puntiagudo 37 F2
Cerro Puripica 18 C2
Cerro Quebrado 21 G2
Cerro Queitane 13 E2
Cerro Rabi 40 B5
Cerro Ramadita 22 C2
Cerro Redondo (Ant) 18 C1
Cerro Redondo (Ara) 35 F3
Cerro Redondo (Coi) 41 F4
Cerro Río Blanco 29 G5
Cerro Roth 42 A4
Cerro Rucachoroy (A) 35 G3
Cerro Sairecábur (B) 15 H6
Cerros Anallacsi (B) 11 F3
Cerros San Juan 22 C1
Cerros Colorados (A) 21 H5
Cerros de Condoriri 11 E3
Cerros del Guacate 15 E5
Cerros de Lipinza 35 F4
Cerros de Metalqui 36 C5
Cerros de Ramada 23 E4
Cerros de Sunicagua (B) 11 E3
Cerros de Tocorpuri (B) 15 H5
Cerros de Vireira 14 B6
Cerro Seymour 52 C5
Cerro Sichal 15 E3
Cerro Sierra Nevada 21 G6
Cerro Sinalco (B) 13 G5
Cerro Sombrero 49 E6
Cerro Sosneado (A) 29 G6
Cerro Stokes 42 C1
Cerro Tambillos Alto 14 D2
Cerro Tatajachura 13 E2
Cerro Telivilla (B) 13 G3
Cerro Tetas 14 C3
Cerro Toco 18 B1
Cerro Tres Frailes 43 F4
Cerro Tres Picos (A) 37 G5
Cerro Tres Picos (Ais) 41 E6
Cerro Tres Picos (Mag) 51 H3
Cerro Tres Puntas (JF) 19 G5
Cerro Tres Tetas 16 D4
Cerro Triángulo 42 D2
Cerro Tridente 21 G5
Cerro Tronquitos 23 E6
Cerro Tupungato 29 H3
Cerro Unita 12 C3
Cerro Uyupani (B) 11 F5
Cerro Valenzuela 51 G2
Cerro Ventarrón 12 C5
Cerro Ventarrones 16 D5
Cerro Vicuña Mackenna 16 D5
Cerro Vilacollo 10 D6
Cerro Violeta 52 D4
Cerro Walkyrenstein 42 C6
Cerro Yaretas 29 G2
Cerro Yate 37 F4
Cerro Yeso 29 G6
Chaca 10 B6
Chacance 14 D5
Chacao 36 D4
Chacarilla 13 E5

Chacay 25 F6
Chacayal 34 C6
Chacay Alto 25 E3
Chacayes 29 G4
Chacritas 22 B5
Chadmo Central 38 C1
Chaitén 39 E1
Chalaco 27 E5
Chalinga 24 D6
Chalinguita 27 E4
Challacota (B) 13 H2
Chamiza 37 E3
Champa 29 F4
Champulli 34 D6
Chanabaya 12 B6
Chañar (Coq) 25 E2
Chañar (Coq) 25 E4
Chañar (Coq) 25 F5
Chañaral 20 B5
Chañaral Alto 27 E1
Chañaral de Carén 27 E1
Chañar Blanco 22 B6
Chañarcillo 22 C3
Chanchan 32 B4
Chanco 30 B4
Chanleufu 34 D3
Chanquiuque 30 C2
Chapa Verde 29 F5
Chaparano 37 F4
Chapilca Varillar 25 F4
Chapiquiña 10 D4
Charaña (B) 10 D2
Charrúa 32 D2
Chaschuil (A) 23 H3
Chaulico 36 D1
Chaurahue 36 D5
Chellepín 27 E4
Chépica 31 E1
Chepu 36 C4
Cherquenco 35 E1
Chiapa 13 E2
Chigualoco 26 C4
Chiguana (B) 15 H1
Chiguayante 32 C2
Chijo 13 F2
Chilcaya 11 E6
Chile Chico 41 G5
Chilita 10 D6
Chillán 30 C2
Chimbarongo 29 E6
Chimbero 22 D1
China Creek 52 D1
Chinchillani 11 F6
Chincolco 27 E5
Chipana 14 B2
Chipaya (B) 11 H6
Chiquero (A) 27 H5
Chironta 10 C4
Chirre 34 D6
Chislluma 10 C3
Chiuchiu 15 F5
Choapa 26 D4
Chocalán 29 E4
Cholchol 32 C6
Cholgo 37 F4
Cholguán 33 E2
Cholila (A) 37 H6
Chonchi 36 C6
Choquecota (B) 11 H4
Choroico 32 C3
Chorombo 29 E3
Choros Bajos 24 D2
Chorrillo Solitario (A) 48 B2
Choshuenco 35 E4
Chovellen 30 B4
Chucuyo 11 E4
Chulluncane 13 F3
Chulo 22 D2

Chumildén 37 E6
Chungará 11 E4
Chungungo 24 D3
Chuqicamata 15 E5
Chuquiananta 10 D3
Chusmisa 13 E3
Chuyaquen 36 D3
Cifuncho 20 B3
Cinto (P) 10 A2
Ciruelos (Ohi) 28 C6
Ciruelos (Lag) 34 D3
Cisnes Medio 39 F5
Cobija 14 B5
Cobquecura 30 B5
Cocalán 29 E5
Cochamó 37 F3
Cochiguas 25 F5
Cochrane 43 G1
Codegua 29 F5
Codegua 31 F1
Codpa 10 C6
Coelemu 30 B6
Cogotí 27 E2
Cohihueco 35 E4
Coihaique 41 G2
Coihaique Alto 41 H2
Coihue 32 D3
Coihueco 30 D6
Coimuvao 30 B5
Coinco (Ohi) 29 E5
Coinco (Lag) 38 D1
Coipasa (B) 13 G1
Coipín 30 C6
Coipué 30 C2
Coirón 27 E4
Colbún 31 E4
Colcha (B) 13 H6
Colchane 13 F1
Colcura 32 B2
Colegual 36 D2
Colin 30 D3
Colina 29 F2
Collacagua 13 F4
Collaguasi 13 F6
Colliguay 29 E2
Collihuinco 36 D2
Collipulli 32 D5
Colmo 28 D1
Colón 29 F5
Colonia 32 D3
Colonia Lautaro 32 C6
Colorado 25 G4
Colpitas 10 D3
Coltauco 29 E5
Comalle 31 E1
Combarbalá 27 E2
Comodoro Py (A) 48 A3
Complejo Eléctrico Futaleufú (A) 39 G1
Complejo Los Libertadores 29 G1
Compu 36 C6
Comuy 34 D2
Conai 30 B6
Coñaripe 35 E3
Conay 25 G1
Concepción 32 C1
Conchali 26 D4
Conchi 15 F4
Conchi Viejo 15 F4
Concón 28 D1
Concordia 36 D2
Condoriaco 25 E3
Confluencia 30 B6
Constitución 30 B3
Contaco 34 B6
Contao 37 E4
Contulmo 32 B5
Copaquilla 10 D4

Copaquiri 13 F6
Copiapó 22 C2
Copihue 30 D5
Copiuilemu 32 C1
Coposo 32 C3
Coquiao 36 C4
Coquimbo 24 D4
Coral 31 E3
Corcovado (A) 39 G2
Cordillera Darwin 52 C5-D6
Cordillera de Ansilta (A) 27 G3
Cordillera de Claudio Gay 21 G6
Cordillera de Colangüil (A) 25 H4
Cordillera de Domeyko 17 G3-H2
Cordillera de la Costa 14 B3
Cordillera de la Puntilla 25 F3
Cordillera de la Ramada (A) 27 G5
Cordillera de los Patos del Norte (A) 25 G6
Cordillera del Romero 25 E2
Cordillera del Tigre (A) 27 H5
Cordillera de Mahuicanchi 34 C2-3
Cordillera de Manrique (A) 27 G2-H2
Cordillera de Nahuelbuta 32 B4-5
Cordillera de Paine 45 F6
Cordillera de Pirulil 38 B1-C1
Cordillera de Polcura 33 F3-G2
Cordillera de Puichén 36 C5-6
Cordillera Doña Ana 25 G3-4
Cordillera Doña Rosa 25 F6
Cordillera Litrancura 33 F5
Cordillera Nevada 35 E6
Cordillera Olivares (A) 25 H6
Cordillera Pemehue 33 E4-F5
Cordillera Pinto 47 G4-5
Cordillera Riesco 47 H6
Cordillera Sarmiento de Gamboa 47 E2-3
Cordillera Serrucho 47 G6
Cordillera Vidal 47 H4
Cordón de la Totora (A) 27 G2
Cordón de Puntas Negras 18 C3-4
Cordón Esmeralda 43 G1
Cordón Marchant 39 E4
Corinto 30 D3
Corneche 28 D4
Coronel (Mau) 30 B5
Coronel (Bio) 32 B2
Coronel Alcérreca 10 C4
Corral 34 B4
Corralones 31 E3
Corral Quemado (Coq) 25 E5
Corral Quemado (San) 29 G3
Correntoso 37 E3
Correntoso (A) 37 G1
Cortadera (Ata) 22 D4
Cortadera (Coq) 25 E4
Cortadera (A) 23 H3
Corte Alto 36 D2
Cortiduría 30 D3
Cosapa (B) 11 F4
Cosapilla 10 D3
Coscaya 13 E3
Coya 29 F5
Coy Aike (A) 48 D1
Coya Sur 14 D5
Cruce Las Arañas 28 D4
Crucero 36 D1
Cruces 34 C3
Cruz Grande 24 D3
Cuaico 30 C5
Cuarto Chorrillo 49 E6
Cucao 36 C6
Cudico 34 C5
Cueva Fell 48 D4
Cueva Pali Aike 48 D4
Cui (B) 13 G5

Culenar 31 F3
Culenco 32 C3
Cullén 49 E6
Cultivos (A) 31 G6
Cululil 36 C3
Cumbres de San Gregorio 48 C5
Cumpeo 31 E3
Cunaco 29 E6
Cunamo 34 C6
Cunco 35 E2
Cuncumén (Coq) 27 F4
Cuncumén (San) 28 D4
Cuñibal 32 C3
Curacautín 33 E6
Curacaví 29 E3
Curaco 32 D5
Curaco de Vélez 36 D5
Curahuanga de Carangas (B) 11 G3
Curahue 36 C6
Curanilahue 32 B3
Curanipe 30 B4
Curarrehue 35 F3
Curepto 30 C2
Curicó 31 E2
Curiñanco 34 C4
Cuya 12 B1
Cuz Cuz 26 D3

Dalcahue 36 D5
Degán 36 C5
Detif 36 D6
Diaguitas 25 F4
Dichato 30 A6
Diego de Almagro 20 D5
Dinamarqueros 48 B5
Diuquín 32 C3
Dollinco 34 D4
Dollinco 34 D5
Domeyko 25 E1
Doñihue 29 E5
Dorotea 47 G2
Duao 30 D3

El Abanico 33 F3
El Alambrado 35 E1
El Álamo 33 E3
El Algarrobo 24 D6
El Amargo 33 E5
El Arco 37 F3
El Arrayán 29 F3
El Avellano 32 D5
El Barraco 37 F3
El Boldo 32 B3
El Bolsón 36 D1
El Bolsón (A) 37 G4
El Bosque 25 F5
El Calafate (A) 45 G4
El Canelo 29 G3
El Carmen (Ata) 20 C5
El Carmen (Ohi) 28 D5
El Carmen (Bio) 33 E1
El Carpintero 29 E2
El Carrizo (Ata) 22 D5
El Carrizo (Ata) 25 F2
El Centinela (A) 45 G5
El Chacay 33 F3
El Chaitén (A) 45 F1
El Cholar (A) 33 H3
El Churque 25 E3
El Cobre (Coq) 24 D5
El Cobre (Val) 26 D6
El Cobre (Val) 27 E6
El Colorado (San) 29 G2
El Colorado (San) 31 E3
El Convento 28 D4
El Corral 25 F2
El Crucero 34 D6
El Desierto 17 E3

El Duraznito 25 F2
Elena (A) 39 H3
El Encanto 37 F1
El Guaico 30 D1
El Guanaco 21 E1
El Hoble 34 C6
El Huachi 33 E4
El Huecú (A) 33 H4
El Ingenio 26 D6
Elisa de Borda 22 D3
El Islón 24 D4
El Islote 37 F1
Elizalde 41 G3
El Jardín 21 E5
El Latiguillo 31 E5
El Maitén 41 E6
El Maitén (A) 37 H4
El Manzanito 29 G4
El Manzano (Ara) 35 E1
El Manzano (Maga) 48 A5
El Manzano (Ohi) 28 D5
El Maqui 27 F1
El Médano 16 C6
El Melocotón 29 G4
El Melón 26 D6
El Membrillo 29 E4
El Mirador 34 B5
El Molle 25 E4
El Monte 29 E4
El Morado 24 D1
El Morro 33 E5
El Natre 34 D1
El Ñilhué 27 E6
El Palenque (A) 35 H2
El Palomar (A) 33 H1
El Palqui 25 E6
El Pangue (Coq) 25 E6
El Pangue (San) 29 E2
El Parrón 30 C5
El Peñón 24 D4
El Perallito 24 D5
El Pidén 25 G5
El Planchón 31 G2
El Portezuelo (A) 41 H4
El Progreso 32 C3
El Puestito (A) 27 H5
El Quisco 28 D3
El Romero (Ata) 22 B6
El Romeral (Coq) 24 D3
El Romero (Coq) 24 D4
El Romero (Coq) 25 E4
El Romeral (Ohi) 31 F1
El Salado 20 C5
El Salto 31 F4
El Salvador 21 E5
El Sauce 30 D6
El Sifón 26 D5
El Tabo 28 D3
El Tambo (Coq) 25 E4
El Tambo (Coq) 27 E4
El Tangue 24 C5
El Tártaro 27 E6
El Tatio 15 H5
El Terrón 22 C6
El Toco 28 D6
El Tofo 24 D3
El Toro 33 F3
El Tránsito (Ata) 25 F1
El Tránsito (San) 29 F4
El Tránsito (Mau) 30 D5
El Trebolar 29 E2
El Turbio (A) 47 G2
El Turco 28 D3
El Volcán (Ata) 23 F2
El Volcán (San) 29 G4
El Zurdo (A) 48 A3
Embalse Bullileo 31 E5
Embalse Cogotí 27 E2

Embalse de Caritaya 10 D6
Embalse Digua 30 D5
Embalse El Yeso 29 G4
Embalse Huechún 29 F2
Embalse Las Paloma 25 E6
Embalse Machicura 31 E4
Embalse Rapel 28 D5
Embalse Recoleta 25 E5
Empalme 34 C5
Empedrado 30 C3
Enco 35 E4
Endesa 31 F4
Engorda 26 D5
Enquelga 13 F1
Ensenada 37 E2
Ensenada Chaitén 39 E1
Ensenada Mar Gruesa 24 C6
Ensenada San Blas 46 B2
Ensenada Toltén (JF) 19 E6
Ensenada Totoralillo 26 C5
Ensueño 16 C3
Entre Lagos 34 D6
Entre Vientos 48 A6
Epuyén (A) 37 H5
Ercilla 32 D5
Escalera 14 B4
Escalerilla 14 D1
Escuadrón 32 B2
Esmeralda (Ant) 14 C6
Esmeralda (Ant) 20 B4
Esmeralda (San) 29 F2
Esmeralda (Val) 28 D3
Esperanza (Ohi) 28 D5
Esperanza (Bio) 33 E1
Esperanza (A) 48 B1
Espíritu Santo 26 D2
Esquel (A) 39 H1
Esquiña 10 D6
Estación Cocharcas 30 C6
Estación El Toco 14 D4
Estación Enconche 21 E5
Estación Experimental de Pintados
   12 D5
Estancia Alicura (A) 35 H6
Estancia Avelina 48 B5
Estancia Bella Vista (A) 48 B3
Estancia Bombalot 48 A4
Estancia Buenos Aires (A) 53 G4
Estancia Cabo Buen Tiempo (A)
   49 E2
Estancia Cabo San Pablo (A) 53 H5
Estancia Carmen (A) 53 F5
Estancia Castillo (A) 53 E3
Estancia Cauchicol (A) 53 F3
Estancia Chacabuco (A) 35 G6
Estancia Chimen Aike (A) 49 E3
Estancia Ciaike 48 C4
Estancia Corral de Piedra (A) 35 H6
Estancia Cullen (A) 49 F6
Estancia Dalmacia 52 C2
Estancia de Manzanas (A) 35 G4
Estancia Despedida (A) 53 F4
Estancia El Falso (A) 48 D1
Estancia Esperanza (A) 53 F5
Estancia Flora (A) 48 C1
Estancia Guairabo 52 A2
Estancia Guakenken Aike (A) 48 D2
Estancia Invierno 47 H6
Estancia Kark 47 G1
Estancia La Angelina (A) 49 E2
Estancia La Blanca (A) 45 H3
Estancia La Carolina (A) 48 C1
Estancia La Celestina (A) 53 H5
Estancia La Fe (A) 48 D1
Estancia La Federica (A) 43 G6
Estancia Lago Rico (A) 45 F5
Estancia Lago Roca (A) 45 F5
Estancia La Langosta (A) 45 H1

Estancia La Portada 48 C4
Estancia Las Buitreras (A) 48 C3
Estancia Las Chinas 45 G6
Estancia La Vanguardia (A) 48 B1
Estancia La Vega 48 C4
Estancia Llaneza (A) 43 H6
Estancia Los Pozos (A) 49 E2
Estancia Los Robles (A) 53 F4
Estancia Mamuil Malal (A) 35 G4
Estancia María Behety 53 F3
Estancia Menéndez (A) 53 F3
Estancia Moy Aike Chico (A) 48 D1
Estancia Moy Aike Grande (A) 48 D1
Estancia Oazy Harbour 48 B5
Estancia Ponsonby 47 H5
Estancia Punta Alta (A) 47 H2
Estancia Punta del Lago (A) 45 H2
Estancia Punta Loyola (A) 49 E3
Estancia Rancahue (A) 35 H3
Estancia Río Fuego (A) 53 G4
Estancia Río Grande 52 D3
Estancia Río Irigoyen (A) 53 H5
Estancia Río Tranquilo (A) 47 G3
Estancia Rivadavia (A) 53 G5
Estancia Rocallosa 47 H5
Estancia Russfin 52 D3
Estancia San Ernesto (A) 45 F4
Estancia San Gregorio 48 C5
Estancia San Jorge 48 C4
Estancia San José (A) 45 F2
Estancia Santa Rosa (A) 35 H3
Estancia Sara (A) 53 F2
Estancia Sarita 48 C6
Estancia Sarmiento 53 F4
Estancia Springhill 48 D5
Estancia Tepi (A) 53 G4
Estancia Tinogasta (A) 53 G4
Estancia Tucu Tucu (A) 43 H4
Estancia Verano 47 H5
Estancia Victorina 45 F6
Estancia Vicuña 53 E4
Estancia Wagner 48 A5
Estero Alhué 29 E4
Estero Alicahue 27 E5
Estero Antivero 29 F4
Estero Camisas 27 E4
Estero Casablanca 28 D2
Estero Chimparongo 31 E1
Estero Codegua 29 F5
Estero de Chocalán 29 E4
Estero de Nilahue 28 C6
Estero de Puangue 29 E3
Estero de Quinahue 30 D1
Estero de Upeo 31 F2
Estero de Yali 28 D4
Estero Falcón 44 D2
Estero Gulrvilo 28 D6
Estero Las Palmas 27 E5
Estero Lolol 28 D6
Estero los Puercos 30 D3
Estero Millahue 26 D3
Estero Punitaqui 26 D1
Estero Pupio 26 D4
Estero Quitralco 41 E3
Estero Reloncaví 37 F3
Estero Rosario 28 C5
Estero San Miguel 28 C6
Estero Temuco 33 E2
Estero Tircahue 31 E3
Estero Topocalma 28 C5
Estero Valle Hermoso 27 E2
Estero Vichuquén 30 C1
Estique (P) 10 C2
Estrecho de Magallanes 47 E6
Estrecho Nelson 46 B2
Estuario Silva Palma 51 G1
Ex Oficina Alemania 20 D2
Ex Oficina Chile 20 D2

Falso Cabo de Hornos 55 F3
Farellón Suárez 27 E3
Farellones 29 G3
Finca de Chañaral 20 D6
Fiordo Alejandro 40 B4
Fiordo Asia 45 E5
Fiordo Burns 40 B3
Fiordo Comau o Leptepu 37 F5
Fiordo Cornish 40 B4
Fiordo Cupquelán 41 E4
Fiordo Elefantes 40 D4
Fiordo Hoppner 40 A5
Fiordo Largo 37 F6
Fiordo Newman 40 B5
Fiordo Peel 44 D6
Fiordo San Esteban 40 B4
Fiordo Steffen 43 E2
Flor del Desierto 17 F2
Florida 32 C1
Folilco 34 D4
Fray Jorge 24 C6
Freire 34 D2
Freirina 22 B6
Fresia 36 D2
Frutillar 37 E2
Fuerte Bulnes 52 A2
Futaleufú 39 G2
Futrono 35 E5

Gallegos Chico 48 B4
Galvarino 32 C6
General Cruz 32 D2
General Lagos 10 D2
General López 36 D1
General Pérez (B) 11 E2
Golfo Almirante Montt 47 F3
Golfo Corcovado 38 D1-2
Golfo Coronados 36 C3
Golfo de Ancud 37 E4
Golfo de Arauco 32 B2
Golfo de Penas 40 B6
Golfo Ladrillero 44 A1
Golfo San Esteban 40 C6
Golfo Sarmiento de Gamboa 46 B4
Golfo Tres Montes 40 B5
Golfo Trinidad 44 A3
Golfo Xaultegua 51 E1
Gorbea 34 D2
Granalla 37 E6
Graneros 29 F5
Granizo 29 E2
Grupe Theo 46 D5
Grupo Camden 51 G6
Grupo Carmela 46 C2
Grupo Desertores 37 E6
Grupo Gómez Carreño 46 D2
Grupo Lobos 46 C2
Grupo Narborough 46 C5
Grupo Solari 46 D1
Guabún 36 C4
Guachacalla (B) 11 G6
Guadaba 32 C5
Guaillamarca (B) 11 H3
Gualcuna 25 E3
Guallali 33 F5
Guallatiri 11 E5
Gualleco 30 C2
Gualligua 25 E4
Gualpin 34 C2
Gualve 30 C5
Guamalata 24 D6
Guampulla 25 E5
Guañacagua 10 C6
Guanaco (A) 33 H3
Guanaqueros 24 D5
Guanaquillo 16 D1
Guangualí 26 D5
Guanillos 14 B2

Guanta 25 F4
Guasquiña 12 D3
Guatacondo 13 E6
Guatín 15 H6
Guatral 37 E3
Guatulame 27 E1
Guaviña 12 D3
Guayacán 29 G3
Guayasca 36 C1
Guer Aike (A) 48 D2
Gultro 29 F5
Guzmán 34 D6

Hacienda Castilla 22 B4
Hanga Roa (EI) 19 F2
Hanga Vinapu (EI) 19 F3
Helo Sur 35 E1
Hermanos Clark 29 G1
Hidango 28 C5
Hidroeléctrica Montandón 21 E5
Hierro Viejo 27 E5
Higuerita 25 E3
Higueritas 24 D5
Hijuelas 29 E1
Hilarios 14 D2
Horcón 26 D6
Hornitos 14 B6
Horno 27 E4
Hornopirén 37 F4
Hospital 29 F4
Hostería Río Penitente 48 A4
Hotel Carpa 48 A5
Hotel Río Rubens 47 H3
Hotel Tres Pasos 47 G2
Huachacaya (B) 11 G6
Huachipato 32 B1
Hualañé 30 D2
Hualqui 32 C2
Huanara (P) 10 A1
Huape 30 C6
Huara 12 C4
Huasco 22 A5
Huasco Bajo 22 A5
Huaychoca (B) 11 F5
Hueicolla 34 B5
Huellelhue 34 C4
Huelquén 29 F4
Huemul 31 F1
Huentelauquén 26 C3
Huépil 33 E3
Huequecura 35 E5
Huequén 32 C4
Hueyusca 36 D2
Huife 35 F2
Huildad 38 D1
Huilinco 34 C6
Huilma 36 D1
Huinay 37 F5
Huinganes 30 C3
Huintil 27 E3
Huiscapi 35 E3
Huite (Lag) 34 D4
Huite (Lag) 36 D4
Humapalca 10 C3
Hurtado 25 E3

Icalma 35 G1
Iglesia Colorada 22 D4
Ilabaya (P) 10 A2
Ilihue 35 E5
Illapel 26 D3
Iloca 30 C2
Ilque 37 E3
Imilac 17 G5
Inacaliri 15 H4
Inca de Oro 20 D6
Incahuasi 25 E2
Independencia del Parque (A) 39 G1

Ingeniero Barriga 26 D4
Ingeniero Capps (A) 48 B3
Ingeniero Santa María 26 D5
Inspector Fernández 32 D5
Iquique 12 B4
Isla Aguirre 51 G5
Isla Agustín 46 B1
Isla Alberto Vargas 43 E3
Isla Aldea 42 B5
Isla Alejandro Selkirk 19 E6
Isla Anafur 44 C4
Isla Angamos 42 B6
Isla Angelotti 46 C2
Isla Apiao 36 D6
Isla Arthur 38 B4
Isla Arturo 44 A1
Isla Ascensión 38 C3
Isla Atilio 38 D4
Isla Auchilu 40 C2
Isla Ayautau 42 C2
Isla Barrios 43 E3
Isla Barros Arana 46 D4
Isla Basket 51 H6
Isla Bayly 55 F3
Isla Benjamín 38 C5
Isla Betecoi 38 C4
Isla Blanca 42 B3
Isla Bolados 38 C5
Isla Bordes 46 D4
Isla Boxer 42 C5
Isla Breaksea 42 A3
Isla Briceño 43 E3
Isla Broken 38 B5
Isla Butachauques 37 E5
Isla Byron 42 B2
Isla Cabrales 42 A5
Isla Cailín 38 D2
Isla Caldcleugh 42 D4
Isla Caldera 47 E5
Isla Camel 44 C3
Isla Campana 42 B4
Isla Canning 44 C4
Isla Capitán Aracena 51 H4
Isla Caracciollo 44 B4
Isla Carlos (Mag) 42 A6
Isla Carlos (Mag) 51 E4
Isla Carlos III 51 F2
Isla Carolina 54 C2
Isla Carrington 46 D2
Isla Caucahue 36 D5
Isla Cayetano 51 G3
Isla Central 43 F5
Isla Chaculay 40 D1
Isla Chaffers 38 C4
Isla Chañaral 24 C1
Isla Chatham 44 C5
Isla Childs 50 D2
Isla Chipan 44 B1
Isla Choros 24 C2
Isla Chulín 37 E6
Isla Chungungo 24 D3
Isla Churrecue 40 D2
Isla Clarence 51 G4
Isla Clemente 40 C2
Isla Concoto 38 C4
Isla Cóndor 46 D5
Isla Contreras 46 C3
Isla Cook 52 B6
Isla Corso 44 B3
Isla Covadonga 42 A6
Isla Crosslet 40 B5
Isla Cuptana 38 C5
Isla Dagnino 46 C1
Isla Damas 24 C2
Isla Daroch 46 C2
Isla Darwin 52 B6
Isla Dawson 52 B3-B4
Isla Deceit 55 G4

Isla del Guindo 28 D6
Isla de Maipo 29 E4
Isla Desierta 40 B1
Isla Desolación 46 D6
Isla Diego 51 H4
Isla Diego de Almagro 46 B2
Isla Djenana 46 C4
Isla Doña 44 B5
Isla Dring 40 C1
Isla Drummond Hay 44 C4
Isla Dumont D'Urville 54 D2
Isla Duque de York 44 B5
Isla Ekyira 38 D4
Isla Escribano 44 B4
Isla Esmeralda 42 A6
Isla Esperanza 44 D6
Isla Ester 38 D6
Isla Evans (Mag) 46 D1
Isla Evans (Mag) 50 D2
Isla Farquhar 42 C4
Isla Farrel 44 C5-6
Isla Figueroa 44 C4
Isla Filomena 38 D5
Isla Fitz Roy 40 D3
Isla Francisco (Ais) 38 D5
Isla Francisco (Ais) 43 E3
Isla Freire 46 D5
Isla Fresia 34 D6
Isla Freycinet 55 G3
Isla Frodden 44 B6
Isla Froilán 44 C5
Isla Furia 51 G5
Isla Gable (A) 53 G6
Isla Garcia 38 D4
Isla Garrao 38 C5-D5
Isla Garrido 40 C2
Isla Gaviota 24 D2
Isla Goicolea 38 C4
Isla Gordon 52 C6
Isla Grande (Ata) 22 B2
Isla Grande (Mag) 47 G6
Isla Grande de Chiloé 36 B5
Isla Grande de Tierra del Fuego
   52 D3
Isla Gran Guaiteca 38 C3
Isla Graves 50 C1
Isla Grevy 55 F3
Isla Guafo 38 B3
Isla Guamblin 38 A6
Isla Guapi 35 E5
Isla Guar 37 E4
Isla Guardián Brito 51 F4
Isla Guarello 44 B4
Isla Guerrero 40 C3
Isla Hall 55 G4
Isla Hannover 44 C6
Isla Henderson 54 D3
Isla Hereford 40 B5
Isla Herschel 55 G4
Isla Hillyar 42 C5
Isla Hornos 55 G4
Isla Hoste 54 D1
Isla Huemules 40 D3
Isla Humos 40 D2
Isla Hunter 47 E3
Isla Ilabella 51 E4
Isla Inocentes 44 C5
Isla Ipún 38 B5
Isla Isquiliac 40 C2
Isla Izazo 38 C5
Isla James (Ais) 38 C6
Isla James (Mag) 51 E4
Isla Jaques 51 E1
Isla Javier 40 B6-C6
Isla Jechica 38 C5
Isla Jesús 38 C6
Isla Johnson 38 B5
Isla Jorge (Ais) 38 C6

Isla Jorge (Mag) 44 C4
Isla Jorge Montt 46 C1
Isla Juan Guillermos 46 D4
Isla Juan Stuven 42 B3
Isla Kalau 44 A2
Isla Kempe 51 F5
Isla Kent 38 B6
Isla King 46 C4
Isla Knor 42 B5
Isla Laitec 38 D2
Isla Latorre 46 D5
Isla Lemu 40 C1
Isla Lemuy 36 D6
Isla Lennox 55 G2
Isla Leucaype 38 D4
Isla Level 38 B5
Isla L'Hermite 55 F4
Isla Libertad 51 E4
Isla Liebre 38 B6
Isla Linlín 36 D5
Isla Little Wellington 42 C5
Isla Llancahue 37 E5
Isla Llenihuenu 38 B4
Isla London 51 G6
Isla Londonderry 52 A6
Isla Lort 51 F4
Isla Luff 55 H2
Isla Luz 40 D2
Isla Macías 41 F5
Isla Madre de Dios 44 B4
Isla Magdalena 39 E5
Isla Maillén 37 E3
Isla Maldonado 46 C3
Isla Malleras 38 B4
Isla Malvinen 44 C2
Isla Manuel 39 E5
Isla Manuel Rodríguez 47 E5
Isla Matilde 40 C2
Isla Mechuque 36 D5
Isla Melchor 38 C6
Isla Merino Jarpa 42 D3
Isla Metalqui 36 C5
Isla Meulín 36 D5
Isla Middle (Ais) 42 C4
Isla Middle (Mag) 55 G3
Isla Midhurst 38 B4
Isla Millar 42 C3
Isla Mocha 32 A6
Isla Montague 44 A1
Isla Mornington 44 B2
Isla Mortimer 51 G4
Isla Morton 54 D3
Isla Mukchen 38 D4
Isla Muñoz 46 D4
Isla Nalcayec 40 D3
Isla Navarino 55 F1
Isla Negra 28 D3
Isla Newton 47 E3
Isla Noir 51 E5
Isla Nueva 55 H2
Isla Núñez 50 D2
Isla O'Brien 52 B6
Isla Ofhidro 42 D4
Isla Olga 54 B1
Isla Orella 42 B6
Isla Orlebar 42 C3
Isla Owen 47 E1
Isla Pacheco 46 C4
Isla Pan de Azúcar 20 B4
Isla Parker 46 D5
Isla Patricio Lynch 42 A5
Isla Paz 38 B6
Isla Pedro Montt 46 D4
Isla Petters 44 B1
Isla Piazzi 46 D3
Isla Picton 55 H1
Isla Pilot 44 B3
Isla Porcia 42 C3

Isla Prat 42 B4
Isla Presidente González Videla
   44 C6
Isla Providencia 47 E6
Isla Puduguapi 39 E1
Isla Puluqui 37 E4
Isla Purcell 40 C6
Isla Quehue 36 D6
Isla Quemada 40 D2
Isla Queullín 37 E4
Isla Quihua 36 D4
Isla Quilán 38 C2
Isla Quinchao 36 D6
Isla Quiriquina 30 A6
Isla Ramírez 46 B3
Isla Recalada 50 C2
Isla Refugio 38 D4
Isla Riesco 47 G6
Isla Riquelme 42 B5
Isla Rivero 40 C2
Isla Robert 44 C5
Isla Robinson Crusoe (JF) 19 G5
Isla Rojas (Ais) 38 C5
Isla Rojas (Ais) 40 D2
Isla Rosas 46 D4
Isla Rowlett 38 B6
Islas Agnes 51 F5
Isla Salas 40 C3
Isla Sala y Gómez 20 A4
Isla San Ambrosio 20 B3
Isla San Félix 20 A2
Isla San José 40 D3
Isla San Pedro (Lag) 38 C2
Isla San Pedro (Ais) 42 B2
Isla Santa Clara (JF) 19 G6
Isla Santa Inés 51 F3
Isla Santa María (Ant) 16 C2
Isla Santa María (Bio) 32 B2
Isla Sara 50 D1
Isla Saumarez 44 D2
Islas Bajas 38 C4
Islas Barnevelt 55 G4
Islas Beauclert 50 D1
Islas Chaigneau 46 C4
Islas Chauques 36 D5
Isla Schlucht 42 C4
Islas Christmas 54 C2
Isla Scout 42 C3
Islas Crafton 51 E4
Islas Diego Ramírez 54 D5-6
Isla Desambre 55 G2
Islas Evout 55 H3
Islas Fincham 50 D3
Islas Forsyth 38 B4
Islas Gilbert 51 H6
Islas Idelfonso 54 C3
Isla Sidney 51 G6
Isla Silva Renard 46 D4
Isla Simpson 40 D3
Islas Jungfrauen 42 B3
Islas Las Huichas 40 D1
Islas Los Quincheles 38 D4
Islas Magill 51 F5
Isla Solar 44 B6
Isla Sombrero 42 C2
Islas Puyo 40 B2
Islas Rennell 46 D3
Islas Rice Trevor 50 D2
Isla Stanley 51 G4
Isla Staveley 46 C5
Isla Stewart 51 H6
Isla Stokes 38 B5
Isla Stosch 42 B6
Islas Vallenar 40 B1
Islas Wollaston 55 G3
Islas Wood 54 C2
Isla Tabón 36 D4
Isla Tac 37 E5

Isla Taggart 44 A2
Isla Tahuenahuec 38 C5
Isla Talcán 37 E6
Isla Tamar 47 E6
Isla Taraba 46 D3
Isla Tarlton 44 B4
Isla Tenquehuén 40 B2
Isla Teresa (Ais) 38 C6
Isla Teresa (Ais) 43 E3
Isla Terhalten 55 G2
Isla Thompson 52 B6
Isla Tilgo 24 D3
Isla Tomas 54 C2
Isla Topar 44 C3
Isla Traiguén 40 D2
Isla Tranqui 38 D1
Isla Tránsito 38 D6
Isla Tres Dedos 40 C1
Isla Tuamapu 38 B4
Isla Tuap 38 D6
Isla Usborne 40 B4
Isla Valverde 38 C4
Isla Vancouver 46 D1
Isla Van der Meulen 42 C4
Isla Verdugo 38 D4
Isla Vicente 42 C2
Isla Vickham 52 B4
Isla Victoria 40 D1
Isla Vidal Gormaz 46 C3
Isla Videla 42 B5
Isla Virtudes 46 C2
Isla Wager 42 B2
Isla Waller 40 A5
Isla Waterman 54 C2
Isla Wellington (Mag) 42 C6
Isla Wellington (Mag) 44 C1
Isla Willams 38 B6
Isla Williams 42 D5
Isla Yerbas Buenas 46 D5
Isla Zañartu 47 E5
Isla Zealous 42 C3
Islote Blanco 20 B6
Islote El Verdugo (JF) 19 H5
Islote Juanango (JF) 19 G5
Islote Los Chamelos (JF) 19 H5
Islotes Evangelistas 46 B5-C5
Islotes Pájaros 24 C2
Islote Vinillo (JF) 19 G5
Isluga 13 F1
Istmo de Ofqui 40 C5
Itahue 31 E2
Itisa 10 D5

Jagüe (A) 23 H6
Jaramillo (A) 39 H3
Jauja 13 E4
Jayocote (B) 11 G5
J Dufour 12 D2
José Francisco Vergara 14 D5
Juan López 16 C2
Juan Soldado 24 D4
Julia 17 F2
Junín 12 B3
Junín de los Andes (A) 35 G4
Junquillar 30 C3
Junta 34 C5
Junta de Chingoles 25 E3
Juntas 25 G4

Katterfeld 39 G6
Kerber 47 H4
Kimiri Aike 48 D5

La Abundancia 21 E6
La Aguada 26 D1
La Angostura (A) 35 H2
La Arena (Ata) 25 F1
La Arena (Coq) 25 F6

La Atravesadera (A) 35 H2
La Baja 43 F2
La Barra 34 B5
La Boca 32 B1
La Cabaña 39 F2
La Calera 29 E1
Lacalle 17 E5
La Canabina 27 F6
La Capilla (Bio) 30 D6
La Capilla (Ara) 32 D5
La Cascada 12 D4
La Cebolla 23 E2
La Chimba 24 D6
La Colonia 43 F1
La Compañía 24 D4
La Compañía 29 F5
La Cruz (Val) 29 E1
La Cruz (San) 29 E5
La Cumbre 29 F1
La Disputada 29 G2
La Dupont 15 E5
La Estrella 28 D5
La Exploradora 21 E4
La Fontaine (A) 33 G4
La Fortuna 17 F2
Lago Abascal 37 F5
Lago Alegre 43 G3
Lago Aluminé (A) 35 G2
Lago Amalia (A) 53 E3
Lago Amutui Quimei (A) 39 G1
Lago Anibal Pinto 47 G3
Lago Antuk (A) 53 G5
Lago Argentino (A) 45 G4
Lago Azul 37 G4
Lago Balmaceda 47 G3
Lago Bayo 41 E4
Lago Belgrano (A) 43 H3
Lago Bello 52 D1
Lago Bertrand 41 F6
Lago Blanco (A) 41 H3
Lago Blanco 52 D4
Lago Bórquez 43 E4
Lago Briceño 43 G4
Lago Briox 47 F1
Lago Buenos Aires (A) 41 H4
Lago Burmeister (A) 43 H3
Lago Cabral (A) 43 H6
Lago Caburga 35 F2
Lago Calafquén 35 E3
Lago Caro 41 F3
Lago Castor 41 G2
Lago Cayutué 37 F2
Lago Chacabuco 43 G1
Lago Chaiguaco 38 C1
Lago Chaiguata 38 C2
Lago Chapo 37 F3
Lago Cheepelmuth (A) 53 G5
Lago Chico 52 D4
Lago Cholila (A) 37 G5
Lago Christie 43 G3
Lago Chungará 11 E4
Lago Claro 41 E2
Lago Cochrane 41 G6
Lago Colico 35 E2
Lago Cóndor 41 E2
Lago Conguillio 35 F1
Lago Constancia 35 F6
Lago Copa 39 E6
Lago Correntoso (A) 35 F6
Lago Coyte 41 H1
Lago Cronómetro 39 H2
Lago Cucao 36 C6
Lago Curruhué (A) 35 F4
Lago de Coipasa (B) 13 H1
Lago de Grey 45 F6
Lago de las Rocas 37 G4
Lago de las Torres 39 F6
Lago de los Palos 41 F1

Lago del Sello (A) 41 H6
Lago del Toro 47 F1
Lago de Natri 36 C6
Lago Deseada 52 B1
Lago Deseado 53 E5
Lago Diana 47 G3
Lago Dickson 45 F6
Lago Dulcinea (A) 45 H6
Lago Elena 40 B4
Lago Elizalde 41 F2
Lago Ellis 41 E2
Lago Epuyén (A) 37 H5
Lago Escondido 39 E6
Lago Esmeralda 43 G1
Lago Espolón 39 F2
Lago Esquel (A) 39 H1
Lago Fagnano (Kami) (A) 53 F5
Lago Falkner (A) 35 F6
Lago Fontana (A) 39 G6
Lago Fuego (A) 53 G4
Lago Futalaufquen (A) 37 G6
Lago Galletué 35 G1
Lago General Carrera 41 F5
Lago General Vintter (A) 39 G4
Lago Grande (A) 45 H4
Lago Gris 35 F6
Lago Guillelmo (A) 37 H3
Lago Gutiérrez (A) 37 H2
Lago Hermoso (A) 35 F6
Lago Huechulafquen (A) 35 G4
Lago Huelipilún 35 E2
Lago Huillinco 36 C6
Lago Huishue 35 E6
Lago Icalma 35 G1
Lago Interior 37 F6
Lago Jeinement 41 G5
Lago J. Roca (A) 37 G3
Lago Kruger (A) 37 G6
Lago Lácar (A) 35 F5
Lago La Paloma (A) 41 G3
Lago La Plata 39 F6
Lago Lapparent 41 G4
Lago Largo 41 G1
Lago Llanquihue 37 E2
Lago Lleulleu 32 B5
Lago Lolog (A) 35 F5
Lago Lynch 52 D4
Lago Maihue 35 E5
Lago Martín (A) 37 G3
Lago Mascardi (A) 37 G2
Lago Meliquina (A) 35 G6
Lago Menéndez (A) 37 G6
Lago Mercedes 53 E3
Lago Meullin 41 E1
Lago Nahuel Huapi (A) 37 H2
Lago Nansen (A) 43 H3
Lago Navarino 55 G1
Lago Neltume 35 E4
Lago Nordenskjöld 45 F6
Lago O'Higgins 43 F5
Lago Paguipulli 35 E4
Lago Palena 39 G3
Lago Palique 45 H6
Lago Pampa Alta 41 H1
Lago Peilaifa 35 F3
Lago Pirihueico 35 F4
Lago Pollux 41 G2
Lago Portales 41 F2
Lago Porteño 47 F1
Lago Posadas (A) 43 H2
Lago Presidente Ríos 40 C4
Lago Presidente Roosevelt 39 F6
Lago Puelo (A) 37 G5
Lago Pueyrredón (A) 43 H1
Lago Puyehue 35 E6
Lago Quetru 43 F3
Lago Quillén (A) 35 G3
Lago Ranco (Lag) 34 D5

Lago Ranco 34 D5
Lago Reñihue 37 F6
Lago Riesco 41 F2
Lago Riñihue 35 E4
Lago Risopatrón 39 E4
Lago Rivadavia (A) 37 G6
Lago Roca (A) 45 F5
Lago Rosario 39 H2
Lago Rosselot 39 F4
Lago Rupanco 37 E1
Lago San Antonio 38 C1
Lago San Martín (A) 43 G6
Lago Sarmiento (A) 45 H5
Lago Sarmiento 45 F6
Lagos de la Pascua (A) 53 E2
Lago Situación (A) 39 G1
Lago Sofía 47 G2
Lago Steffen (A) 37 G3
Lago Tagua Tagua 37 F3
Lago Tannhauser (A) 45 F3
Lago Tar (A) 43 H6
Lago Tarahuin 36 C6, 38 C1
Lago Tepuhueco 36 C6
Lago Todos Los Santos 37 F2
Lago Trafül (A) 35 G6
Lago Trinidad 34 B5
Lago Tromen (A) 35 G3
Lago Tyndall 47 F1
Lago Verde (A) 41 H4
Lago Verde (Ais) 39 G4
Lago Verde 39 F4
Lago Vichuquén 30 C1
Lago Viedma (A) 45 H3
Lago Viedma (A) 45 F2-H2
Lago Villarica 35 E2
Lago Windhond 55 F2
Lago Yehuin (A) 53 F5
Lago Yelcho 39 F2
Lago Yulton 39 E6
Lago Zenteno 41 F2
La Guaica 12 D5
La Guanaca 21 E6
Laguani (B) 13 G6
La Guardia 23 E3
Laguna Agrio (A) 33 G5
Laguna Amarga 45 F6
Laguna Aricota (P) 10 A1
Laguna Azul 45 F6
Laguna Barco 33 G5
Laguna Bismarck (A) 48 D3
Laguna Blanca (Tar) 10 D2
Laguna Blanca (Mag) 48 A5
Laguna Brava (A) 23 G5
Laguna Budi 34 C1
Laguna Cabeza del Mar 48 B6
Laguna Cari Lauquen (A) 31 G6
Laguna Casimiro 48 B5
Laguna Cauquenes 29 F5
Laguna Chaxa 18 A2
Laguna Colbún 31 E4
Laguna Colorado (A) 48 B3
Laguna Colorado (B) 15 H4
Laguna Cóndor (A) 47 H3
Laguna Cotacotani 11 E4
Laguna de Aculeo 29 E4
Laguna de Batuco 29 F2
Laguna de Colorados (A) 21 H4
Laguna de la Azufrera 21 G1
Laguna de la Invernada 31 F4
Laguna de la Laja 33 G2
Laguna del Inca 29 G1
Laguna del Maule 31 G5
Laguna del Negro Francisco 23 F3
Laguna de Los Cisnes 52 B1
Laguna de los Patos (A) 21 H3
Laguna del Toro 48 A4-5
Laguna de Matanzas 28 D4
Laguna de Pescado (A) 53 G5

Laguna Dial 31 F6
Laguna Diamante (A) 29 H5
Laguna Ema 52 D2
Laguna Escondida 21 G6
Laguna Esperanza (A) 47 H1
Laguna Fea (A) 31 G5
Laguna Isola Bella (A) 48 C2
Laguna La Leona (A) 48 D2
Laguna Lanalhue 32 B5
Laguna Larga 48 B4
Laguna Larga (A) 47 H3
Laguna La Rubia (A) 45 H2
Laguna Lejía 18 B3
Laguna Malleco 33 E5
Laguna Miñiques 18 B3
Laguna Miscanti 18 B3
Laguna Mucalliri (B) 13 G2
Laguna Negra (A) 31 G5
Laguna Negra 29 G3
Laguna Pali Aike (A) 48 C3
Laguna Parinacota 13 E1
Laguna Pastos Grandes (B) 15 H3
Laguna Peñuelas 28 D2
Laguna Potrok Aike (A) 48 C3
Laguna Quepe 33 E6
Laguna Riesco 47 G6
Laguna Salada (A) 48 B1
Laguna San Rafael 40 D5
Laguna Santa Rosa 23 F1
Lagunas Bravas 15 G5
Lagunas de Epulafquén (A) 33 G1
Lagunas de Morro Gay (A) 48 A3
Lagunas de Teno 31 G2
Laguna Seca (A) 49 E2
Laguna Serrano 52 B1
Laguna Talar 18 B4
Laguna Tapo Aike (A) 45 H6
Laguna Tara 18 D1
Laguna Torca 30 C1
Laguna Travesía (A) 47 H1
Laguna Tuyajto 18 C4
Laguna Varvarco Campos (A) 31 F6
Laguna Verde (A) 23 G3
Laguna Verde (B) 15 H6
Laguna Verde (Val) 28 D2
Laguna Verde (Ata) 23 H1
Laguna Verde (Ara) 35 F1
Laguna Verde (Mag) 52 B1
Laguna Vergara 52 D1
Laguna Villacota (P) 10 B1
Lagunillas 28 D3
La Herradura 24 D4
La Higuera (Ata) 22 C6
La Higuera (Coq) 24 D3
La Higuera (Ata) 25 F1
La Higuera (Coq) 25 E4
La Hoyada 22 C5
La Junta (Ata) 23 F2
La Junta (Ais) 39 F4
La Junta (Mag) 47 G3
La Laguna 25 F2
La Laja 32 C3
La Leonera (Ohi) 29 F5
La Leonera (Lag) 34 D3
La Ligua (Val) 26 D6
La Ligua (Coq) 27 E1
Lambert 24 D4
La Mina 31 F4
La Montaña 31 F2
La Mora 27 E6
Lampa 29 E2
Lanalhue 32 B4
Lanco 34 D4
La Negra 16 D3
La Obra 29 F3
La Ola 21 F5
La Orilla de Auquinco 31 E1
La Pampa (Ant) 20 D2

La Pampa (Coq) 25 E3
La Pampa (Ata) 25 G1
La Parva 29 G2
Lapataia (A) 53 E6
La Paz 34 D3
La Peña (Bio) 33 F4
La Peña (Lag) 34 C5
La Picada 37 F2
La Pita 30 B5
Lapito 32 D4
La Placilla 26 D1
La Pólvora 21 E3
La Poza (Lag) 37 E2
La Poza (Lag) 37 E4
La Puerta 23 E2
La Punilla 33 F1
La Punta 29 F4
La Quema 43 F2
Laraquete 32 B2
Laredo 27 E1
La Retuca 28 D2
La Rioja 17 E1
Larmahue 29 E6
La Roroya 25 G4
La Rosa 29 E5
Larraín Alcalde 28 C6
La Rufina 31 G1
Lasana 15 F4
Las Bombas 20 C4
Las Breas (Coq) 25 F2
Las Breas (Coq) 25 F5
Las Cabras 28 D5
Las Campanas 30 C4
Las Cañas (Coq) 26 D4
Las Cañas (Mau) 30 B3
Las Cardas 24 D5
Las Cascadas 37 E2
Las Coloradas (A) 35 H3
Las Condes 29 F3
Las Cruces (Ant) 16 C2
Las Cruces (Val) 28 D3
Las Cuevas 10 D4
Las Cuevas (A) 29 G1
Las Damas 28 C5
Las Dichas 28 D2
Las Empanadas (A) 23 H4
La Serena 24 D4
Las Garzas (Mau) 30 C4
Las Garzas (Mau) 31 F4
Las Horquetas (A) 48 C2
Las Hortensias 35 E2
Las Juntas (Ata) 22 D4
Las Juntas (Coq) 25 E6
Las Lagunas (A) 33 G2
Las Lajas (A) 33 H6
Las Leñas (A) 31 H2
Las Mariposas 29 E4
Las Melosas 29 G4
Las Nieves 29 F6
La Sombra 33 E6
Las Ovejas (A) 33 H2
Las Palmas (Coq) 26 C2
Las Palmas (Val) 26 D5
Las Palmas (Ohi) 31 E1
Las Pampas (A) 39 G4
Las Pircas 27 E3
Las Placetas 25 F4
Las Quemas (Lag) 34 C6
Las Quemas (Lag) 36 D3
Las Quilas 30 B5
Las Raíces 30 B5
Las Ramadas 27 F2
Las Rojas 25 F1
Las Rosas 30 C5
Las Sosas 24 D6
Las Tablas 28 D2
Lastarria 34 D3
Las Vacas 26 D4

Las Varas (P) 10 A3
Las Viñas 32 D4
Lata 16 D3
La Tapera 39 G5
La Tirana 12 D5
La Torre 24 D6
Latorre 16 D2
La Trinchera 30 C2
La Unión 34 C5
Lautaro (Ata) 22 D4
Lautaro (Ara) 32 D6
La Ventana (A) 31 G3
La Viña 27 E6
La Yarada (P) 10 A4
Lebú 32 A4
Leleque (A) 37 H5
Lenca 37 E3
Lepa (A) 37 H6
Lepoy 33 F5
Leptepú 37 F5
Lequena 15 F2
Leyda 28 D3
Lican Ray 35 E3
Lihueimo 28 D6
Limache 29 E2
Limáhuida 26 D4
Limarí 24 D6
Limpa 27 E4
Linao 36 D4
Linares 30 D4
Lincantén 30 C2
Linderos 29 F4
Linzor 15 H4
Lipimávida 30 C1
Lipingue 34 D4
Liquiñe 35 F4
Lirima 13 F3
Litpampa 26 D2
Litú 30 D2
Litueche 28 C5
Liucura 32 D1
Livilcar 10 C5
Llahuin 27 E2
Llaillay 29 E1
Llampos 22 D2
Llanada Grande 37 G4
Llancacura 34 C5
Llano Blanco 33 E4
Llano de la Paciencia 17 H3
Llano de Martínez 22 D3
Llano de Pajonal 22 B6
Llanos 17 E3
Llanos de Guanta 25 F4
Llanquihue 37 E2
Llanta 20 D5
Llao Llao (A) 37 G2
Lleguiman 37 E4
Llepo 31 E4
Llica (B) 13 G3
Llico (Mau) 30 C1
Llico (Bio) 32 A2
Llifén 35 E5
Llimpo 27 E4
Lloicaco 30 B6
Llolleo 28 D3
Llonquen 35 F4
Lloyca 28 D4
Lo Barnechea 29 F3
Lo Chacón 29 E4
Locumba (P) 10 A2
Lo Gallardo 28 D3
Lolcura 36 D3
Lolenco (San) 29 E3
Lolenco (Ara) 32 D4
Lolol 30 D1
Loma Colorada 32 B2
Lomacura 35 F1
Lomas Bayas (Ant) 17 F2

Lomas Bayas (Ata) 22 D4
Lo Miranda 29 E5
Loncoche 34 D3
Loncomilla 36 D5
Loncopangue 33 F4
Loncopue (A) 33 H5
Loncotoro 36 D2
Longaví 30 D5
Longotoma 26 D5
Longoyito 28 D5
Lonquimay 33 F6
Lontué 31 E2
Lo Orosco 28 D2
Lora 30 C2
Los Álamos 32 B4
Los Andes 29 F1
Los Ángeles 32 D3
Los Antiguos (A) 41 H5
Los Arroyos (A) 31 H2
Los Azules (Ata) 23 E2
Los Azules (Coq) 26 D4
Los Baños 24 C6
Los Baños (P) 10 A4
Los Barros 33 G3
Los Brujos 33 E4
Los Chañares 25 G1
Los Colorados 22 B5
Los Conales 34 C5
Los Dones 14 C6
Los Erizos (A) 27 F4
Los Guindos 29 E4
Los Hornos 24 D3
Los Lagos 34 D4
Los Laureles 35 E2
Los Lirios 29 F5
Los Llanos 27 E1
Los Llolles 35 E5
Los Lobitos 24 D2
Los Loros 22 D4
Los Maitenes 29 G3
Los Maquis 29 F6
Los Molles 26 D5
Los Molles (A) 31 H2
Los Morros 25 F2
Los Morros (A) 31 H2
Los Muermos 36 D3
Los Nabos 30 C4
Los Niches 31 E2
Los Peladeros 27 E4
Los Pellines 37 E2
Los Peumos 30 C2
Los Placeres 16 D2
Los Prados 33 E6
Los Puquios 31 E6
Los Queltehues 29 G4
Los Queñes 31 F2
Los Rabones 31 E4
Los Ranchones 28 C5
Los Riscos (Lag) 36 D1
Los Riscos (Lag) 37 E2
Los Rulos 29 E3
Los Sauces 32 C5
Los Tallos 34 D4
Los Ulmos 34 C5
Los Vagabundos 43 F2
Los Vientos 17 E6
Los Vilos 26 C4
Lota 32 B2
Lo Valdés 29 G4
Lo Valdivia (Ohi) 28 C6
Lo Valdivia (Mau) 31 E2
Lo Vásquez 28 D2
Lumaco 32 C5

Macaya 13 E4
Machalí 29 F5
Máfil 34 C4
Maicolpué 34 B6

Maipo 29 F4
Maipú 29 F3
Maitencillo (Ata) 22 B6
Maitencillo (Coq) 24 D5
Maitencillo (Coq) 26 C1
Maitenes 33 F5
Maitenrehue 32 C4
Majadillas 31 E2
Majadita (A) 25 H5
Malalcahuello 33 F6
Malalhue 34 D3
Mallin (A) 31 H5
Mallín Grande 41 F5
Malloco 29 E3
Mallos 29 E6
Malvilla 28 D3
Mandinga 28 D4
Mañihuales 41 G1
Manquemapu 36 C1
Mantos Blancos 16 D2
Mantos de Hornillos 26 C2
Mantos de la Luna 14 B4
Manzanar 33 F6
Manzano 33 F5
Maray 24 D3
Marchihue 28 D6
Margarita (Ata) 22 C2
Margarita (Ata) 22 C2
María Elena 14 C5
María Emilia 49 F6
María Pinto 29 E3
María Sofía 47 G4
Maricunga 21 F6
Mariquina 34 D3
Martínez de Rosas 34 D2
Matancilla (Coq) 25 F3
Matancilla (Coq) 26 D3
Matancilla (Coq) 27 E3
Matanzas 28 C4
Matao 36 D6
Mataquito 30 D2
Matilla 12 D5
Mauce 28 D1
Maule 30 D3
Maullín 36 D3
Maunga Otu (EI) 19 F2
Maunga Pukatikei (EI) 19 H2
Maunga Terevaja (EI) 19 F1
Maunga Tuutapu (EI) 19 F2
Mauque 13 E2
Mauro 27 E4
Medina 31 E4
Mehuin 34 C3
Mejillones 16 C1
Mela 30 B6
Melado 31 E4
Melefquén 35 E3
Melinka 38 C3
Melipeuco 35 F1
Melipilla 29 E4
Melirupo 32 B3
Mellizos 15 E6
Melozal 30 D2
Membrillo 30 D5
Menque 30 A6
Merceditas 22 C5
Metrenco 34 D1
Mialqui 25 E6
Michilla 14 B6
Millantú 32 D3
Millantue 34 B6
Mina Algarrobo 22 B6
Mina Caracoles 15 E2
Mina Carbón Pecket 48 A6
Mina del Indio 25 G4
Mina Dichosa 20 C5
Mina El Inglés 29 E5
Mina El Rosario 27 E5

Mina El Toqui 39 G6
Mina Fakir 14 B2
Mina La Casualidad (A) 21 H2
Mina La Coipa 21 F6
Mina La Escondida 17 G5
Mina La Estrella 20 C4
Mina La Juanita 29 G5
Mina Loreto 52 A1
Mina Marte 23 F2
Mina Punta de Lobos 12 B6
Mina Rosario 20 C4
Mina San Manuel 20 C5
Minas de Toquepala (P) 10 A1
Minas Las Hediondas 25 G4
Mincha 26 D3
Minetué 35 F1
Mininco 32 D4
Miñimiñi 12 C1
Miñita 12 D1
Miño 15 F1
Miraflores (Ata) 22 B5
Miraflores (Mau) 30 D4
Miraflores (Lag) 36 C6
Mirasol 28 D2
Mision Fagnano (A) 53 G5
Misquihue 36 D3
Mocha 12 D3
Mocopulli 36 C5
Molco 30 C4
Molina 31 E2
Molino 30 C4
Molinos 10 C4
Mondaca (A) 25 H5
Monte Águila 32 D2
Monte Aymond 48 D4
Monte Chaltel o Fitz Roy 45 F1
Monte Muela 51 G2
Montenegro 29 F2
Monte O'Higgins 44 D2
Monte Oscuro 31 F2
Monte Patria 25 E6
Monte Pissis (A) 23 G4
Monte San Lorenzo o Cochrane
43 G2
Monte San Valentín o San Clem-
ente 41 E5
Monte Tronador (A) 37 G2
Monturaqui 17 H5
Monumento Natural Alerce Costero
34 B5
Monumento Natural Contulmo
32 B5
Monumento Natural Cueva del
Milodón 47 G2
Monumento Natural Dos Lagunas
41 G2
Monumento Natural Laguna de los
Cisnes 52 B1
Monumento Natural La Portada
16 C3
Monumento Natural Los Pingüinos
48 B6
Monumento Natural Pichasca 25 E5
Monumento Natural Salar de Surire
11 E6
Moquegua 30 C3
Morrillos 25 E5
Morrito de Chara 13 F6
Morro Chico 48 A4
Morro Mejillones 16 C1
Morza 31 F1
Mostazal 21 E6
Motu Iti (EI) 19 F3
Motu Kao Kao (EI) 19 F3
Motu Marotiri (EI) 19 H2
Motu Nui (EI) 19 F3
Motu Tautara (EI) 19 F2
Mulchén 32 D4

Mulluri 11 E6
Muñoz 25 G5

Nacimiento 32 C3
Nahuelbuta 32 B5
Nahuel Huapi (A) 37 H2
Nahueltoro 30 D6
Nama 12 D1
Nancagua 29 E6
Ñanco 32 D5
Ñancul (Ara) 35 E3
Ñancul (Ara) 34 D4
Nantoco 22 D3
Nasahuento 10 D3
Navidad 28 C4
Negreiros 12 C3
Negrete 32 D3
Nehuentue 34 C1
Neltume 35 F4
Nerquihue 28 D6
Neurara 17 H4
Nevado de Incahuasi 23 H1
Nevado de Longaví 31 E5
Nevado de San Francisco 23 H1
Nevado de Tres Cruces 23 G2
Nevado El Fraile 23 H1
Nevados de Chillán 33 F2-G2
Nevados de Putre 10 D4
Niblinto 30 D6
Niebla 34 C4
Nilahue 28 C6
Ninhue 30 C6
Ninquihue 30 C6
Ñipas 30 B6
Ñiquén 30 D5
Ñirehuao 41 H1
Nirivilo 30 C3
Nogales 26 D6
Ñorquin (A) 33 H4
North Ridge (A) 49 E4
Nueva Aldea 30 B6
Nueva Braunau 37 E3
Nueva Elqui 25 G4
Nueva Esperanza 34 D6
Nueva Imperial 34 C1
Nueva Toltén 34 C2

Observatorio Astronómico El Tololo
25 E5
Observatorio Cerro Morado 25 E5
Observatorio Las Campanas 25 E2
Observatorio La Silla 25 E2
Ocoa 29 E1
Oficina Chacabuco 17 E1
Oficina Flor de Chile 20 D2
Oficina Humberstone 12 C4
Oficina Santa Laura 12 C4
Oficina Victoria 12 C6
O'Higgins 16 D3
Ojeda 14 C4
Olivar Alto 29 F5
Ollagüe 15 G1
Olmué 29 E1
Onaisín 52 D2
Opoqueri (B) 11 H5
Orongo (EI) 19 F3
Osorno 34 C6
Otárola 24 C5
Ovahe (EI) 19 G1
Ovalle 24 D6

Pabellón (Ata) 22 D3
Pabellón (Coq) 25 F6
Pabellón (San) 29 E4
Pacarisa (B) 11 G6
Pachia (P) 10 B3
Pachica (Tar) 10 C6
Pachica (Tar) 12 D3

Pachingo 24 C6
Pacoma 13 G2
Padre Hurtado 29 F3
Paguantalla (B) 13 G2
Paicavi 32 B4
Paiguano 25 F4
Pailahueque 32 D5
Pailimo 28 C5
Paillaco (Val) 32 B5
Paillaco (Lag) 34 D5
Paine 29 F4
Paipote 22 C2
Paiquiña 14 B1
Palena 39 G3
Palermo 32 D3
Palermo Aike (A) 48 D3
Palestina 17 E3
Palhuen 30 C2
Palinco 32 C2
Palmilla (Ohi) 28 D6
Palmilla (Mau) 30 D4
Palo Blanco 25 E2
Palos Quemados 26 D6
Palqui 36 D5
Pama 27 E2
Pampa Alona 13 E5
Pampa Amarilla (A) 29 G2-H2
Pampa Arturo Prat 16 D3
Pampa Blanca 12 C6
Pampa Columtucsa 13 E4-F3
Pampa Cruz Verde (P) 10 A3
Pampa de Camarones 10 B6
Pampa de Chaca 10 B5
Pampa de Chiza 12 C1
Pampa del Asador (A) 43 H3
Pampa de las Zorras 12 B6-C6
Pampa del Avestruz 15 F3
Pampa del Indio Muerto 14 D5-6
Pampa de Loncoloan (A) 35 G1-H1
Pampa de los Bayos (A) 21 H5
Pampa del Tamarugal (Tar)
12 C3-D5
Pampa del Tamarugal (Ant)
15 E3-E5
Pampa de Oxaya 10 C5-D5
Pampa de Tana 12 B2
Pampa Elvira 17 F3-G3
Pampa Engañadura 12 C6
Pampa Higualue 35 F5
Pampa Huasco 13 F4
Pampa Miraje 14 B5
Pampa Moctezuma 15 E5
Pampa Ossa 10 C4
Pampa Perdiz 12 C4
Pampa San Juan 20 D3
Pampa Soledad 14 D2
Pampa Tres Arroyos (A) 31 G6
Panavinto 13 F2
Pan de Azúcar (Ant) 17 H4
Pan de Azúcar (Coq) 25 E4
Pangal (Ohi) 29 F5
Pangal (Lag) 36 C3
Pangue 25 F5
Panguilemo 30 D3
Panguipulli 35 E4
Paniahue 28 D6
Panimávida 31 E4
Panitao 37 E3
Panquehue 29 F1
Pantanillos 30 C3
Panulcillo 24 D6
Papal 43 F2
Paposo 20 C1
Papudo 26 D6
Paraguay 36 D2
Parca 13 E4
Parcohaylla 11 E6
Paredones 28 C6

Parga 36 D2
Pargua 36 D4
Parinacota 11 E4
Parque Inglés 31 F3
Parque Nacional Alberto de Agostini 52 B5
Parque Nacional Alerce Andino 37 F3
Parque Nacional Archipiélago de Juan Fernández 19 F5
Parque Nacional Bernardo O'Higgins 42 D4
Parque Nacional Cabo de Hornos 55 G3
Parque Nacional Chiloé 36 C5
Parque Nacional Conguillío 35 F1
Parque Nacional El Morado 29 G4
Parque Nacional Francisco Perito Moreno (A) 43 G3
Parque Nacional Fray Jorge 24 C6
Parque Nacional Hornopirén 37 F4
Parque Nacional Huerquehue 35 F2
Parque Nacional Isla Guamblín 38 A6
Parque Nacional Isla Magdalena 39 E5
Parque Nacional Isluga 13 E2
Parque Nacional La Campana 29 E2
Parque Nacional Lago Palena 39 G3
Parque Nacional Laguna del Laja 33 F3
Parque Nacional Laguna San Rafael 40 B5
Parque Nacional Lanin (A) 35 G4
Parque Nacional Lauca 10 D5
Parque Nacional Llanos de Challe 22 A5
Parque Nacional Los Alerces (A) 37 G6
Parque Nacional Los Glaciares (A) 45 F3
Parque Nacional Los Guaitecas 40 C3
Parque Nacional Nahuelbuta 32 C4
Parque Nacional Nevado de Tres Cruces 23 G1
Parque Nacional Pali Aike 48 D4
Parque Nacional Pan de Azúcar 20 B4
Parque Nacional Puyehue 37 F1
Parque Nacional Queulat 39 F5
Parque Nacional Rapa Nui (EI) 19 G2
Parque Nacional Río Simpson 41 G2
Parque Nacional Tolhuaca 33 E5
Parque Nacional Torres del Paine 45 F6
Parque Nacional Vicente Pérez Rosales 37 F2
Parque Nacional Vilches 31 F3
Parque Nacional Villarica 35 F3
Parque Natural Pumalín 37 E6
Parque Provincial Aconcagua (A) 29 H1
Parque Provincial Volcán Tupungato (A) 29 H2
Parral 30 D5
Parronal 30 D2
Paso Aviador Ibáñez 51 F5
Paso Barrancas 31 G5
Paso Boquerón 52 B2
Paso Catrinao 31 F6
Paso Cerro Colorado 31 F6
Paso Cochamo 37 G3
Paso Codorniz 43 G3

Paso Coihaique 41 H2
Paso Columpios 33 G2
Paso de Barahona 25 G6
Paso de Carirriñe 35 F4
Paso de Chollay 25 G2
Paso de Delgado o de la Colorada 27 F1
Paso de Guaitiquina 18 D3
Paso de Icalma 35 G1
Paso de Jama 18 D2
Paso del Agua Negra 25 H5
Paso de la Honda o del Portillo 27 F5
Paso de la Laguna de la Overa (A) 27 F2
Paso de la Laguna Sico 18 D4
Paso del Arco 35 G1
Paso del Bermejo 29 H1
Paso del Indio 44 C1
Paso de Llaima o Santa María 35 G2
Paso del Macho 31 F6
Paso del Medio 42 D2
Paso de los Piuquenes 27 F3
Paso del Planchón 31 G2
Paso del Rincón de la Flecha 23 E6
Paso del Rubio 27 G6
Paso del Verde 27 F2
Paso de Menéndez 37 F6
Paso de Molina 29 G6
Paso de Pelambres 27 F4
Paso de Peña Negra 23 F5
Paso de Pérez Rosales 37 G2
Paso de Pino Hachado 35 G1
Paso de Pircas Negras 23 F4
Paso de Potrerillos 31 G3
Paso de Pucón Mahuida 33 G4
Paso de San Francisco 23 H1
Paso Desecho 33 G3
Paso El Portillo 31 G5
Paso Goree 55 G2
Paso Hondo (Bio) 32 C2
Paso Hondo (Bio) 32 D2
Paso Huahum 35 F5
Paso Inglés 51 G3
Paso Lagunas de Epulafquén 33 G2
Paso Malo 25 G2
Paso Monte Aymond 48 D4
Paso Nevado 31 E4
Paso Nuevo 52 B1
Paso Origen del Río Potrerillos 25 G3
Paso Palena 39 G3
Paso Pehuenche o del Maule 31 G5
Paso Picton 55 G1
Paso Portezuelo Baguales I 45 F5
Paso Portezuelo Baguales IV 45 G5
Paso Richmond 55 H2
Paso Rodolfo Roballos 41 G6
Paso Suroeste 42 B3
Paso Tarleton 46 D2
Paso Trolón 31 G4
Paso Wakefield 51 E4
Pastos Largos 23 E4
Pastos Largos (A) 23 H3
Past River 48 B5
Pataguas 28 D5
Pedegua 27 E5
Pedernales 21 F5
Pedregal 27 E1
Pedregoso 35 E2
Pedro de Valdivia 14 C5
Pedro Montt 20 D5
Pehuén 32 B4
Peine 18 B3
Pejerreyes 24 D5
Pelarco 31 E3
Peldehue 29 F2

Peleco (Bio) 32 B4
Peleco (Ara) 34 C2
Pelequén 29 E6
Pelluhue 30 B4
Pemuco 33 E2
Peña Blanca 20 B6
Peñablanca (Coq) 26 C1
Peñablanca (Val) 28 D2
Peñaflor 29 E3
Pencahue (Ohi) 29 E6
Pencahue (Mau) 30 D3
Penco 32 C1
Península Antonio Varas 47 F2
Península Avellaneda (A) 45 F4
Península Barros Arana 47 F3
Península Brecknock 51 H5
Península Cloué 54 C1
Península Córdoba 51 F1
Península de Brunswick 51 H2
Península de Taitao 40 C4
Península Duende 40 B3
Península Dumas 55 E1
Península Esmeralda 40 C5
Península Exmouth 44 D1
Península Florida 43 G5
Península Forelius 51 H4
Península Greenough 51 H4
Península Hardy 55 E2
Península Juan Mazia 48 C6
Península Larenas 42 C2
Península Magallanes (A) 45 F4
Península Mejillones 16 C2
Península Muñoz Gamero 47 F4
Península Negra 42 C4
Península Pasteur 55 E2
Península Poike (EI) 19 G2
Península Roca 47 F3
Península Rolando 52 A5
Península Rous 54 C2
Península Sisquelan 40 D4
Península Skiring 40 B3
Península Staines 47 E2
Península Swett 42 C3
Península Tres Montes 40 A5
Península Ulloa 51 F2
Península Videau 43 E3
Península Wharton 44 B2
Península Wilcock 44 D5
Península Zach 47 E4
Penita 22 A6
Peñuelas (Coq) 24 D4
Peñuelas (Val) 28 D2
Perales 30 B3
Peralillo 28 D6
Pérez Caldera 29 G2
Perquenco 32 D6
Perquilauquén 30 C4
Perquín 31 E3
Petorca 27 E5
Petrohué 37 F2
Peulla 37 G2
Peumo 29 E6
Pica 12 D5
Pichamán 30 C3
Pichanco 37 F5
Pichasca 25 E5
Pichibudi 30 C1
Pichidangui 26 C5
Pichidegua 28 D6
Pichil 34 C6
Pichilemu 28 C6
Pichipellahuén 32 C6
Pichirropulli 34 D5
Pichi Traful (A) 35 F6
Pidima 32 D5
Pidpid 36 C5
Piedra Colgada 22 C2
Piedra de Águila 32 C4

Piedras Negras 37 F1
Pilhimávida 30 C5
Pillanlelbún 32 D6
Pilpilco 32 B3
Pinguela 25 E1
Pingüinera Seno Otway 48 A6
Pintados 12 D5
Pinto 33 E1
Pintué 29 E4
Piratas 25 E3
Pirca de Villalobos (A) 27 F3
Pirca Las Juntas (A) 27 F3
Pirque 29 F3
Piruquina 36 C5
Pisagua 12 B2
Pisco Elqui 25 F2
Pishuinco 34 C4
Pisiga 13 F2
Pissis 30 B6
Pitrufquén 34 D2
Placilla (Val) 28 D2
Placilla (Ohi) 29 E6
Placilla (Bio) 33 F2
Plato de Sopa 21 G3
Playa Bandurrias 20 C2
Playa Blanca 12 B5
Playa Corazones 10 B5
Playa del Buque Varado (JF) 19 E6
Playa Huáscar 16 C3
Playa Huayquique 12 B4
Playa Larga 19 E6
Playa Negra 32 C1
Playa Peruana 14 B1
Playa Reñaca 28 D1
Playa Sara 20 C2
Población 28 D6
Pocamávida 30 D2
Pocillas 30 C5
Poconchile 10 B5
Polán 15 F2
Polapi 15 G3
Polcura 33 F3
Polloquere 11 E6
Polonia 29 E6
Polpaico 29 E2
Polvaredas (A) 29 H1
Polvo 27 F2
Pomaire 29 E3
Popeta 29 F6
Poroma 13 E3
Portal del Inca 21 E5
Portezuelo 30 B6
Portezuelo Argentino (A) 29 H3
Portezuelo de Chapiquiña 10 D4
Portezuelo de Japu o Caranguillas 11 E5
Portezuelo de las Lágrimas 29 G6
Portezuelo del Cajón 15 H6
Portezuelo de los Patos o Cuesta Colorada 23 G2
Portezuelo de los Piuquenes 29 H3
Portezuelo del Tupungato 29 H3
Portezuelo de Valle Ancho Norte 23 G3
Portezuelo Huemules 41 H3
Portezuelo Llullaillaco 17 H6
Portezuelo Tambo Quemado 11 E4
Portezuelo Vidal Gormaz 23 F3
Portillo 29 G1
Porvenir (Ant) 16 D1
Porvenir (Mag) 52 B2
Posada Conaf 45 F6
Posesión 49 E4
Potrerillos (Ata) 21 E5
Potrerillos (Ata) 25 F2
Potrero Grande 31 F2
Potrero Grande Chico 31 F2
Potrero Seco 22 D3

Punta Roncura 30 C2
Punta Roth 42 A4
Punta Salado 22 B3
Punta Saliente 36 C5
Punta Salinas (JF) 19 H5
Punta San Juan 52 A3
Punta San Juan (El) 19 G1
Punta San Pedro 20 B3
Punta Santa María 52 A2
Punta Sierra 26 C2
Punta Sirena 28 C6
Punta Stockes 44 B6
Punta Sunshine 51 G1
Punta Sur 38 B3
Punta Tablaruca 38 B1
Punta Talca (Coq) 26 C1
Punta Talca (San) 28 D3
Punta Talinay 24 C6
Punta Talquilla 26 C1
Punta Taltal 20 C2
Punta Tames 14 B6
Punta Teatinos 24 D4
Punta Tetas 16 C2
Punta Tiques 38 B2
Punta Tirúa 32 B6
Punta Tomás 26 C3
Punta Topocalma 28 C5
Punta Toro 28 C4
Punta Totoral 22 A4
Punta Tres Cruces 36 D4
Punta Truenos (JF) 19 G5
Punta Tucapel 32 A4
Punta Tunquillax (JF) 19 G5
Punta Urcu 14 B3
Punta Ventana 26 C3
Punta Verde 28 D5
Punta Vial 22 B2
Punta Vicente Porras (JF) 19 E6
Punta Villa Señor 24 C6
Punta Villiers 51 G1
Punta Virgen 26 C2
Punta Weather 38 A3
Punta Yatac 38 D2
Punta Yayes 14 B6
Punta Zenteno 20 B6
Punta Zorra 38 B2
Puntilla (A) 25 H5
Punto Casas (A) 45 G4
Pupio 26 D4
Pupuya 28 C5
Puqueldón 36 C6
Puqui Núñez 12 D5
Puquios (Tar) 10 C4
Puquios (Ant) 13 G6
Puquios (Ata) 22 D2
Purén (Ohi) 29 E5
Purén (Ara) 32 C5
Purey 34 D4
Puringue 34 C3
Puritama 15 H6
Purranque 36 D1
Purrapel 34 D6
Purulón 34 D3
Putaendo 27 E6
Putagán 30 D4
Putina (P) 10 C1
Putrachoique (A) 39 H3
Putre 10 D4
Putú 30 C2

Quebrada Agua Blanca (A) 25 H5
Quebrada Algarrobal 22 C5
Quebrada Ateleura 26 D3
Quebrada Carrizal 22 B4
Quebrada Carrizalillo 22 B5
Quebrada Carrizalillo 22 D3
Quebrada de Aguas Blancas 18 B2
Quebrada de Anchuña 20 C2

Quebrada de Apanza 10 C6
Quebrada de Arcas 15 E3
Quebrada de Aroma (Tar) 12 D3
Quebrada de Aroma (Tar) 13 E2
Quebrada de Azapa 10 C5
Quebrada de Camiña o de Tana
    12 C2
Quebrada de Carrizo 21 E4
Quebrada de Cascabeles 20 C2
Quebrada de Caunani (P) 10 C3
Quebrada de Chanchoquín 22 D6
Quebrada de Chiza 12 B1
Quebrada de Cobani (P) 10 C3
Quebrada de Comaronea 24 D5
Quebrada de Coscaya 13 E3
Quebrada de Curijmalla 10 D6
Quebrada de Escritos (P) 10 C3
Quebrada de Falca (P) 10 B3
Quebrada de Gallinazos o de
    Concordia (P) 10 B4
Quebrada de Garza o Calisama
    10 C6
Quebrada de Guamanga 20 C6
Quebrada de Guanaqueros 17 H5
Quebrada de Guatacondo 13 E6
Quebrada de Hospicio (P) 10 B4
Quebrada de Juncal 20 D4
Quebrada de la Cachina 20 D3
Quebrada del Agua (A) 18 A6
Quebrada de la Higuera 10 C5
Quebrada de Laquillas 21 F2
Quebrada de la Ramada 13 E6
Quebrada del Boquerón 22 B4
Quebrada del Calvario 25 F3
Quebrada del Chaco 21 E2
Quebrada de los Horcones 29 H1
Quebrada del Patón 23 F2
Quebrada del Salado 20 C5
Quebrada del Totoral 22 B4
Quebrada de Matancilla 20 C1
Quebrada de Mejillones 16 D1
Quebrada de Miñimiñi 12 C1
Quebrada de Pachingo 24 C5
Quebrada de Paipote 23 F2
Quebrada de Pastos Largos 21 F6
Quebrada de Putre 10 D4
Quebrada de Quisma 13 E5
Quebrada de Retamilla 12 C2
Quebrada de San Miguel 22 D2
Quebrada de Seca 13 E4
Quebrada de Sichal 15 E2
Quebrada de Soga 12 D2
Quebrada de Sotoca 12 D2
Quebrada de Suca o de Nama
    12 C1
Quebrada de Taltal 20 D2
Quebrada de Tambillo 13 E4
Quebrada de Tarapacá 13 E3
Quebrada de Tocomar 17 G6
Quebrada de Tuina 15 F5
Quebrada de Umallani 10 C6
Quebrada de Vitor 10 C6
Quebrada Doña Inés Chica 20 D4
Quebrada El Perallillo 20 C5
Quebrada El Tabaco 25 F2
Quebrada Espíritu Santo 26 D2
Quebrada Higuerani (P) 10 C3
Quebrada Honda (Coq) 24 D3
Quebrada Honda (Mau) 31 F2
Quebrada Honda 22 A6
Quebrada Las Barrancas 24 D3
Quebrada las Chacras 25 E3
Quebrada Las Llosyas 10 B5
Quebrada Olivares (A) 25 G6
Quebrada Pachuy 25 G2
Quebrada Pan de Azúcar 20 C4
Quebrada Salitrosa o Flamenco
    20 C6

Quebrada San Andrés 23 E1
Quebrada San Juan 22 A6
Quebrada Seca (Coq) 24 C6
Quebrada Seca 25 E6
Quebrada Tignamar 10 D5
Quebrada Tongoicillo 24 D5
Quebrada Vitor 10 B5
Quebradita 25 F6
Quechereguas 32 D5
Quehuita 15 E1
Queilén 36 D6
Queitane 13 E2
Quella 30 C5
Quellón 38 D1
Quellón Viejo 38 D2
Quelón 26 D5
Quelun 26 D3
Quemchi 36 D5
Quenuir 36 C3
Quepe 34 D1
Quetalmahue 36 C4
Queuco 33 F4
Queule 34 C3
Quicavi 36 D5
Quidico (Bio) 32 A3
Quidico (Bio) 32 B5
Quila 37 F3
Quilacahuin 34 C6
Quilaco 33 E4
Quilacoya 32 C2
Quilanto 37 E2
Quilicura 29 F3
Quilimarí 26 D5
Quilitapia 26 D2
Quillagua 14 D3
Quillaico 34 D5
Quilleco 33 E3
Quillén 32 D6
Quillón 32 D1
Quillota 29 E1
Quilpué 28 D2
Quimcahue 28 D4
Quinamávida 31 E4
Quinchamali 30 C6
Quinchilca 34 D4
Quino 32 D6
Quinque 34 C2
Quinquimo 26 D6
Quinta 31 E1
Quinta de Tilcoco 29 E5
Quintay 28 D2
Quintero 28 D1
Quirihue 30 B5
Quiriquina 33 E1
Quitor 15 G6
Quitratué 34 D2
Quiuña 12 C2
Quivolgo 30 C3

Rada Chigualoco 26 C4
Rada Curanipe 30 B4
Rada de Buchupureo 30 B5
Rada de Paposo 20 C1
Rada el Algarrobo 28 D2
Radal 35 E2
Rada Llico 30 C1
Rafael 30 B6
Ralún 37 F3
Ramadilla 23 E4
Ramadillas 32 B3
Ramaditas (Tar) 12 D6
Ramaditas (Coq) 27 E4
Rancagua 29 F5
Rangue 29 E4
Ranguelmo 30 B6
Ranguil 30 D1
Rano Kau (El) 19 F3
Ranquil 30 B6

Ranquil 32 B3
Ranquilco 34 C1
Rapaco 34 C5
Rapel (Coq) 25 E6
Rapel (Ohi) 28 C4
Raqui 32 B3
Rasguñado 43 F2
Rauco 31 E1
Rebeca 31 F1
Recinto 33 F1
Recoleta 24 D6
Refugio Lagunillas 29 G4
Reloca 30 B4
Relún 32 B5
Remehué 34 C6
Reñaca 28 D2
Renaico 32 D4
Rencoret 14 C6
Rengo 29 E6
Requegua 29 E6
Requínoa 29 F5
Rere 32 C2
Reserva Nacional Alacalufes 46 C4
Reserva Nacional Cerro Castillo
    41 G3
Reserva Nacional Coihaique 41 G2
Reserva Nacional El Paposo 16 C6
Reserva Nacional Federico Albert
    30 B4
Reserva Nacional Isla Mocha 32 A6
Reserva Nacional Katalalixar
    42 B4, C2
Reserva Nacional La Chimba 16 C3
Reserva Nacional Lago Cochrane
    41 F6
Reserva Nacional Lago Jeinimeni
    41 H5
Reserva Nacional Lago Rosselot
    39 F4
Reserva Nacional Laguna
    Peñuelas 28 D2
Reserva Nacional Laguna Torca
    30 C1
Reserva Nacional Laguna Varillar
    51 H2
Reserva Nacional Las Chinchillas
    26 D3
Reserva Nacional Las Vicuñas
    11 E5
Reserva Nacional Los Flamencos
    18 A1
Reserva Nacional Los Ruiles 30 B4
Reserva Nacional Magallanes
    51 H1
Reserva Nacional Pampa del
    Tamarugal 12 C3
Reserva Nacional Pampa del
    Tamarugal 12 C5
Reserva Nacional Pingüino de
    Humboldt 24 C2
Reserva Nacional Río Clarillo 29 F4
Reserva Nacional Río Los Cipreses
    29 F6
Resguardo de los Patos 27 F6
Retén Dollinco 33 E6
Retiro 30 D5
Reumén 34 D4
Reunión 32 D2
Riachuelo 36 D1
Riecillos 29 G1
Rihue 32 D4
Rilán 36 D6
Rinconada 29 F1
Rinconada de Guzmán 27 E6
Rinconada de Silva 27 E6
Riñihue 35 E4
Riñinahue 35 E5
Río Abtao 36 C5

Río Agrio (A) 33 H4
Río Agua Negra (A) 25 H5
Río Aluminé (A) 35 G2
Río Amarillo 52 A2
Río Ancoa 31 E4
Río Ansilta (A) 27 H3
Río Arenisca (A) 43 H5
Río Atuel (A) 31 H1
Río Atutia (A) 27 G1
Río Baker 41 F6
Río Barros (B) 11 H6
Río Biobío (Bío) 32 C3, 32 D4
Río Biobío (Ara) 33 F6
Río Blanco (A) 23 F5
Río Blanco (A) 27 G4
Río Blanco (A) 29 H6
Río Blanco (Lag) 37 E2
Río Blanco (Lag) 47 G4
Río Blanco (Val) 29 G1
Río Blanco (Ohi) 29 G5
Río Blanco (Mau) 31 E5
Río Blanco o San Francisco (A)
  25 G6
Río Bote (A) 45 H4
Río Bote (A) 45 H4
Río Bravo 43 F3
Río Bueno (Lag) 34 C5
Río Bueno 34 B5
Río Bulelco 32 B3
Río Burco 33 E4
Río Butalcura 36 C5
Río Cachitos 23 F4
Río Calingasta (A) 27 H3
Río Caloboro 32 B3
Río Camarones 10 C6
Río Canelos 51 H1
Río Cañon 41 F1
Río Capahuira (B) 11 G4
Río Caplina (P) 10 B3
Río Caracoles (A) 43 G5
Río Carampangue 32 B3
Río Caranguillas (B) 11 G3
Río Cariquima 13 F2
Río Carrenleufú (A) 39 H3
Río Catanlil (A) 35 H4
Río Cato 33 F1
Río Caunahue 35 E5
Río Cautín 32 D6,34 C1
Río Cerrado (A) 27 H2
Río Chacabuco 41 F6
Río Chacapoal 29 G5
Río Chacay 25 E6
Río Chaichahuen 34 D6
Río Chaihuin 34 B5
Río Chalinga 27 E3
Río Changaral 30 C6
Río Changomoco (B) 11 F4
Río Chaopa 27 E4
Río Chico 52 D2
Río Chillán 33 F1
Río China Creek 52 D1
Río Chirri 34 D6
Río Cholchol 32 C6
Río Cholguaco 36 C1
Río Cholguán 33 F2
Río Chovellén 30 B4
Río Chubut (A) 37 H5
Río Cisnes (Ais) 39 H5
Río Cisnes 39 F5
Río Clarillo 29 F4
Río Clarillo 29 F6
Río Claro (Mau) 31 E2
Río Claro (Bío) 32 D2
Río Claro 29 E6, 31 F2
Río Claro 31 E3
Río Claro 31 F1
Río Claro 31 F4
Río Claro o Derecho 25 F5

Río Claro Solar 39 F4
Río Cogotí 27 E2
Río Coig (A) 48 D2
Río Coihueco 37 E1
Río Collacagua 13 F4
Río Collón Curá (A) 35 H5
Río Colorado (A) 23 H6
Río Colorado (Val) 29 G1
Río Colorado 27 F6
Río Colorado 29 G3
Río Colorado 31 F3
Río Coluco 36 C5
Río Combarbalá 27 E2
Río Cóndor (A) 45 F2
Río Cóndor 52 C4
Río Contaco 34 B6
Río Copiapó 22 B2-D3
Río Copihuelpi 35 E3
Río Cortaderal 29 G6
Río Cosapa (B) 11 G5
Río Cruces 34 C4
Río Cuanaco (A) 45 G3
Río Culloleo 32 C3
Río Curioso (A) 43 H2
Río Damas 34 D6
Río de Cancosa (B) 13 G3
Río de la Colonia 43 F1
Río de la Invernada 31 G4
Río de la Laguna o Salinas (A)
  27 G3
Río de la Sal (A) 25 H2
Río de las Nieves 41 G5
Río de las Taguas (A) 25 G2
Río de la Troya (A) 23 H4
Río del Carmen 25 F3
Río del Cazadero 22 D6
Río de Leiva 17 F5
Río del Jagüe (A) 23 G5
Río del Medio 23 E5
Río del Medio 25 G3
Río del Oro 48 D6
Río de los Patos (A) 27 H4
Río del Rocín 27 F5
Río del Sobrante 27 E5
Río del Tránsito 22 C6
Río de Montosa 23 E5
Río de Olivares 29 G3
Río Desaguadero (B) 11 H2
Río Diguillín 33 F1
Río Dumo 33 E5
Río Duqueco 33 F3
Río Ecker (A) 41 H6
Río Elqui 25 E4
Río El Volcán 29 H4
Río Fénix Grande (A) 41 H4
Río Figueroa 23 E3
Río Frío (A) 39 G2
Río Frío (Lag) 36 D2
Río Frío 31 F1
Río Frío 39 F3
Río Futa 34 C4
Río Futaleufú 39 F2
Río Gallegos (A) 49 E3
Río Gallegos (A) 48 B3
Río Grande (Ant) 15 G6
Río Grande,(A) 31 G3
Río Grande (A) 53 F3
Río Grande 27 F1
Río Grande 53 E3
Río Guatulame 27 E1
Río Guenguel (A) 41 H3
Río Huaqui 32 D3
Río Huasco 22 B6
Río Hueinahue 35 F5
Río Huelhue 36 C1
Río Hueyusca 36 C2
Río Huichahue 35 E1

Río Hurtado 25 F6
Río Ibáñez 41 F3
Río Illapel 27 E3
Río Iñaque 34 D4
Río Inio 38 C2
Río Isluga 13 F1
Río Itata 30 B6
Río Itatita 33 E3
Río Japón 52 D3
Río Jorquera 23 E4
Río Juncalito 21 F6
Río la Esperanza 32 C4
Río Laguna Grande 22 D6
Río Laja 32 D2
Río la Potranca (A) 45 H1
Río Larqui 33 E1
Río Lauca (B) 11 G5
Río Lauca 11 E5
Río Lavas (A) 43 H6
Río Licán 35 E6
Río Liguay 30 D5
Río Limarí 24 C6
Río Lincauquén 32 B4
Río Lircay 31 E3
Río Lista (A) 43 H3
Río Llico 36 C2
Río Lliuco 36 C1
Río Lluta 10 B4
Río Loa 14 C2, 14 D4, 15 F2
Río Lollelhue 34 D5
Río Lonquén 30 B6
Río Lontué 31 E2
Río López 36 D2
Río Los Choros 24 D2
Río Los Cipreses 29 F6
Río los Fatillos (A) 27 G1
Río Máfil 34 D4
Río Maipo 28 D4, 29 G5
Río Malleco 33 E5
Río Manantiales (A) 27 G2
Río Manflas 22 D5
Río Mañihuales 39 F6
Río Manrique (A) 27 H2
Río Matancillas (A) 27 G3
Río Mataquito 30 D2
Río Maule 30 D3, 31 F4
Río Maullín 36 D3
Río Mauri (B) 11 G1
Río Mayer (A) 43 G5
Río Medina 38 C1
Río Melado 31 E4
Río Melchor (A) 25 G6
Río Mendoza (A) 29 H1
Río Mercedario (A) 27 G5
Río Minco 33 F4
Río Molina 29 G3
Río Mostazal 27 E1
Río Muco 33 E6
Río Mulchén 33 E4
Río Nahue (A) 33 G2
Río Nef 41 E6
Río Negro (A) 27 G2
Río Negro (A) 29 H6
Río Negro (Lag) 36 D1
Río Negro 36 D3
Río Negro 37 E6
Río Neuquén (A) 33 H2-H3
Río Nevado 23 F4
Río Nilahue 35 E6
Río Ñires (A) 43 H4
Río Ñirihuau (A) 37 H2
Río Ñuble 30 D6
Río O'Higgins 52 D1
Río Oro (A) 43 H1
Río Oro 52 C1
Río Oscar 52 C1
Río Palena 39 G3
Río Pangal 29 G5

Río Pascua 43 F4
Río Peladas (A) 23 H2
Río Pellahuén 32 B6
Río Penitente 47 H4
Río Perquilauquén 31 E6
Río Pichay 34 C4
Río Pichileufú (A) 37 H2
Río Pico (A) 39 H4
Río Pico (A) 39 H4
Río Picoiquén 32 C4
Río Pillaguasi (A) 23 H4
Río Pillunleufu 35 E5
Río Pilmaiquén 34 D6
Río Pingueral 32 C1
Río Pinotalca 30 B3
Río Polcura 33 F2
Río Potro 23 E5
Río Primero 25 G3
Río Puelche 31 G4
Río Puelo 37 G4
Río Pulido 23 E4
Río Pulul 33 G6
Río Puntra 36 C4
Río Purapel 30 C4
Río Quiapo 32 B3
Río Quiburcanca 11 E5
Río Quilimari 26 D5
Río Quillén (A) 35 G3
Río Quillén 32 D6
Río Rahue 37 E1
Río Ramadillas 23 E5
Río Ranquil 33 G5
Río Rapel 25 F6
Río Rarinco 32 D3
Río Reloca 30 C4
Río Relún 32 B5
Río Remehue 35 E4
Río Renaico 32 D4
Río Risopatrón 39 F4
Río Roble (A) 43 H3
Río Romera (A) 33 H6
Río Rucue 33 F3
Río Sajama (B) 11 F5
Río Salado (A) 31 H2
Río Salado (Ant) 15 F5
Río Salado (Ant) 15 G6
Río Salado (Ata) 21 E5
Río Sama (P) 10 A3
Río Samo Alto 25 E5
Río Sanaya (B) 11 G6
Río Sancarrón 25 G3
Río San Juan 52 A2
Río San Martín 53 E2
Río San Pedro 15 G4
Río San Salvador 14 D5
Río Seco (Mag) 52 A1
Río Seco (Tar) 10 D4
Río Seco (Coq) 25 G4
Río Simpson 41 G3
Río Sur 37 E3
Río Tarde (A) 43 H2
Río Teno 31 E1
Río Tirúa 32 B6
Río Tinguiririca 28 D6
Río Tinguiririca 31 G1
Río Toconce 15 G5
Río Todos Santos (B) 11 F6
Río Toltén 34 C2
Río Tordillo (A) 31 G2
Río Traiguén 32 D5
Río Trani 34 D5
Río Trocoman (A) 33 H4
Río Tulahuencito 27 F1
Río Tupungato (A) 29 H2
Río Turbio (A) 37 G5
Río Turbio (A) 47 G2
Río Turbio 23 E3
Río Turco (B) 11 G4

Río Valdivia 34 C4
Río Valle del Cura (A) 25 H3
Río Valle Hermoso (A) 27 G1
Río Varvarco (A) 33 H1
Río Verde 47 H5
Río Vergara 32 C4
Río Vilama 15 G6
Río Vilcura 33 F5
Río Villegas (A) 37 H3
Río Vodudahue 37 F6
Río Volcán 27 G5
Río Yelcho 39 E1
Río Zamora 45 G5
Río Zapaleri 18 D1
Río Zapato 52 D3
Ritoque 28 D1
Rivadavia 25 F4
Roa 32 C1
Roblería (Ara) 32 D4
Roblería (Mau) 31 E4
Rocas de Santo Domingo 28 D3
Rocas Norte 54 D5
Rolecha 37 E4
Roma 29 E6
Romeral (San) 29 G4
Romeral (Mau) 31 E2
Rosario 29 E5
Rosario (B) 11 F1
Rucalhué 33 E4
Rucapequén 30 C6
Rucatrar 32 C6
Rungue 29 E2
Rupanco 37 E1

Sabaya (B) 11 G6
Saboya 32 C5
Sagrada Familia 31 E2
Saguara 10 D6
Sajama (B) 11 E4
Saladillo 29 G2
Salala 24 C6
Salamanca 27 E4
Salar Aguas Calientes 21 G1
Salar de Agua Amarga 21 G3
Salar de Aguas Calientes 18 C2
Salar de Aguilar 21 F4
Salar de Arizaro (A) 18 B6
Salar de Ascotán 15 G3
Salar de Atacama 18 A2
Salar de Azufrera 21 G3
Salar de Bellavista 12 C6
Salar de Carcote 15 G2
Salar de Chalviri (B) 15 H6
Salar de Chiguana (B) 15 G1
Salar de Coipasa (B) 13 H2
Salar de Coposa 13 F5
Salar de Empexa (B) 13 F5
Salar de Gorbea 21 G2
Salar de Huasco 13 F4
Salar de Imilac 17 G4
Salar de Incahuasi (A) 18 C5
Salar de Infieles 21 F4
Salar de Jama (A) 18 D2
Salar de Laguani (B) 13 G6
Salar de la Isla 21 G3
Salar de la Laguna (B) 13 G6
Salar de la Laguna Verde (A) 23 G3
Salar de Las Parinas 21 G4
Salar de Llamara 14 C1
Salar del Miraje 14 D5
Salar del Rincón (A) 18 D4
Salar de Maricunga 23 F1
Salar de Navidad 16 D3
Salar de Ollagüe (B) 15 G1
Salar de Pajonales 21 G2
Salar de Pedernales 21 F5
Salar de Piedra Parada 21 G5
Salar de Pintados 12 C5

Salar de Pocitos o Quirón (A) 18 D6
Salar de Pocopoconi (B) 13 G3
Salar de Pujsa 18 C2
Salar de Pular 18 B5
Salar de Río Grande (A) 21 H1
Salar de Seronal 12 C5
Salar de Surire 11 E6
Salar de Talar 18 B4
Salar de Tara 18 D1
Salar de Uyuni (B) 13 H4
Salar Grande 12 C6
Salar Grande 21 G4
Salar Mar Muerto 17 E3
Salar Punta Negra 17 G6
Salar Quisquiro 18 C2
Salar Sur Viejo 12 D6
Salar Wheelwright 21 G6
Salina de Aguas Calientes (A) 21 H3
Salina de la Laguna Verde (A) 23 G2
Salina de Llullaillaco (A) 17 H6
Salinas 17 E1
Salitre (A) 33 H1
Salonas 29 E5
Salto del Agua 34 D3
Salto de la Virgen 41 G2
Salto del Indio 35 E6
Salto del Laja 32 D2
Salto de los Mayores 23 E3
Saltos del Petrohué 37 F2
Sama Grande (P) 10 A3
Samo Alto 25 E5
Samo Bajo 24 D6
San Agustín 27 E4
San Alfonso (San) 29 G4
San Alfonso (Bio) 32 B4
San Antonio (Ata) 22 D4
San Antonio (Mau) 30 C3
San Antonio (Tar) 12 C5
San Antonio (Val) 26 D6
San Antonio (Val) 28 D3
San Bartolo 15 G6
San Bernardo 29 F3
San Carlos 30 C6
San Carlos de Bariloche (A) 37 H2
San Carlos de Purén 32 D4
Sancarrón 25 G3
San Clemente 31 E3
San Cristóbal 17 E3
San Enrique 28 D4
San Esteban 29 F1
San Esteban 30 B4
San Fabián de Alico 30 D6
San Felipe 29 F1
San Félix 25 F1
San Fernando 29 E6
San Francisco de Mostazal 29 F4
San Gabriel 29 G4
San Gregorio 30 D5
San Ignacio (Bio) 30 B6
San Ignacio (Bio) 33 E1
San Javier 30 D3
San Jerónimo 28 D3
San José de Colico 32 B3
San José de la Mariquina 34 C3
San José de Maipo 29 G3
San José de Marchihue 28 D5
San José de Piguchén 27 E6
San Juan (Ant) 17 G1
San Juan (Ant) 20 D3
San Juan (B) 13 H6
San Juan (Lag) 36 D5
San Juan Bautista (JF) 19 H5
San Juan de Pirque 29 F3
San Lorenzo (Coq) 27 E2
San Lorenzo (Val) 27 E6
San Luis 32 D4
San Manuel 28 D4

San Marcos (Tar) 14 B1
San Marcos (Coq) 27 E1
San Martín de Los Andes (A) 35 G5
San Miguel (Tar) 10 B5
San Miguel (Bio) 33 E4
San Nicolás 30 C6
San Pablo (Coq) 25 E4
San Pablo (Lag) 34 C6
San Patricio 35 E1
San Pedro (Ant) 15 F4
San Pedro (Coq) 25 E5
San Pedro (San) 28 D4
San Pedro (Val) 29 E1
San Pedro (Bio) 32 B1
San Pedro (Bio) 32 D2
San Pedro (Lag) 36 C5
San Pedro de Alcántara (Ohi) 30 D1
San Pedro de Atacama (Ant) 15 G6
San Pedro de Atacama 15 G6
San Pedro de Quémez (B) 13 H6
San Pedro de Quiles 26 D1
San Rafael (Mau) 31 E3
San Rafael (Lag) 36 D4
San Ramón (Ata) 22 B2
San Ramón (Lag) 37 E4
San Roque 29 F1
San Rosendo 32 C3
San Sebastián (Val) 28 D3
San Sebastián (Mag) 53 E2
San Sebastián (A) 53 E2
Santa Ana 31 E3
Santa Bárbara 33 E4
Santa Cecilia 26 D2
Santa Clara (Bio) 32 D1
Santa Clara (Bio) 32 D3
Santa Cruz 28 D6
Santa Familia 14 D3
Santa Fé (Ant) 14 D3
Santa Fé (Bio) 32 D3
Santa Filomena 31 E5
Santa Gracia 24 D4
Santa Graciela de Alcones 28 C5
Santa Inés 29 E3
Santa Juana 32 C2
Santa María 29 F1
Santa María del Mar 40 D1
Santa Marta 26 D5
Santa Rosa 12 C4
Santa Rosa de Chena 29 F3
Santa Teresita 47 H4
Santiago 29 F3
Santiago (B) 13 H6
Santuario de la Naturaleza Yerba Loca 29 G2
Santuario El Cañi 35 F2
San Vicente 32 B1
San Vicente de Tagua Tagua 29 E6
Sara de Lebú 32 B4
Sarmiento 31 E1
Sauzal 30 C4
Saya 12 B2
Sección Lazo Balseo 47 F1
Segunda Angostura 48 C6
Selva Oscura 33 E6
Seno Agostini 52 B5
Seno Aisén 41 E24
Seno Almirantazgo 52 C4
Seno Brenton 52 B4
Seno Darwin 52 C6
Seno de las Montañas 47 E3
Seno de Reloncaví 37 F3
Seno Dyneley 51 H4
Seno Dynevo 50 D2
Seno Europa 44 D3
Seno Eyre 44 D1
Seno Franklin 55 F3
Seno Keats 52 A4
Seno Langford 51 E3
Seno Magdalena 52 A4

Seno Otway 47 H6
Seno Owen 52 B4
Seno Penguin 44 D3
Seno Ponsonby 55 E2
Seno Profundo 50 D3
Seno Pulpo 42 C2
Seno Skyring 47 H5
Seno Última Esperanza 47 F2
Seno Unión 47 E4
Seno Ventisquero 39 E5
Sequitor 18 A1
Serón 25 E5
Serrano 20 D6
Sewell 29 G5
S. Fistonic 12 D5
Sibaya 13 E3
Sierra Almeida 17 H4
Sierra Amarilla 16 D6
Sierra Arturo Prat 47 F2
Sierra Banderita 23 E1
Sierra de las Palas 25 G2
Sierra del Cóndor 25 F2
Sierra del Fritis 22 C3-4
Sierra del Jardín 17 F3-4
Sierra del Peñón (A) 23 G5
Sierra del Toro Negro (A) 23 H5
Sierra de Moreno 15 E3
Sierra de Sangra 43 G4-5
Sierra de Setiembre 20 C3
Sierra de Tatulo del Medio 25 G2
Sierra de Valdivieso 52 D5-6
Sierra de Varas 21 F1
Sierra de Vinchina (A) 23 H6
Sierra Dorotea 47 G2
Sierra Gorda 14 D6
Sierra los Colorados 14 C3-4
Sierra Miranda (Ant) 16 D2
Sierra Miranda (Ata) 21 E4-5
Sierra Morena (P) 10 A4
Sierra Overa 20 D3
Sierra Pajonales 22 C1
Sierra Penafiel 17 E6-F6
Sierra Remiendos 16 C5-D5
Sierra Vicuña Mackenna 16 D5-6
Sobraya 10 B5
Socaire 18 B3
Sociedad Chilena El Litio 18 A3
Socompa 17 H5
Socompa (A) 18 A5
Socoroma 10 D4
Soga 12 D2
Soldevila (A) 53 E5
Solor 18 A1
Sondaje 13 E5
Soruco 26 D2
Sotaquí 25 E6
Sotoca 13 E2
Sotomó 37 F3
Suca 12 C1
Surire 11 E6

Tabaqueros 25 E6
Tacna (P) 10 B3
Tacora 10 C3
Tahuinco 27 E4
Taicú 30 B5
Talabre 18 B2
Talagante 29 E4
Talca 30 D3
Talcahuano 32 B1
Talcamávida 32 C2
Talpen 30 C2
Talquipen 30 D6
Taltal 20 C2
Tambería (A) 23 H2
Tambillo 18 B1
Tambillos (Tar) 12 D4
Tambillos (Coq) 24 D5

Tana 12 C2
Tanguao 30 C3
Tanilvoro 33 E1
Tanume 28 C5
Tapi Aike (A) 48 A1
Tapihue 29 E2
Tapihue 30 C4
Tarapacá 12 D3
Tarata (P) 10 B2
Taruguire 10 D6
Teatinos 24 D4
Tegualda 36 D2
Tejería 30 B4
Temuco 34 D1
Tenaún 36 D5
Teno 31 E1
Teodoro Schmidt 34 C2
Terao 36 D6
Termas de Azufre (A) 31 G3
Termas de Catillo 30 D5
Termas de Cauquenes 29 F5
Termas de Chillán 33 F2
Termas de Chusmisa 13 E3
Termas de Colina 29 F2
Termas de Jahuel 27 F6
Termas del Flaco 31 G2
Termas de Llancahue 37 E4
Termas del Plomo 29 H3
Termas de Mamiña 13 E4
Termas de Pemehue 33 F5
Termas de Puyuguapi 39 E5
Termas de Quitralco 41 E2
Termas de Río Blanco 33 F6
Termas de Socos 24 D6
Termas de Tolhuaca 33 E5
Termas El Amarillo 39 F1
Termas El Sosneado (A) 31 H1
Terminal San Gregorio 48 C5
Teupa 36 C6
Tierra Amarilla 22 D3
Tierras Blancas 24 D4
Tignamar 10 D5
Tijeral 32 C4
Tilama 26 D5
Tilcoco 29 E6
Tilomonte 18 A3
Tilopozo 18 A3
Tiltil 29 E2
Timalchaca 10 D5
Timar 10 C5
Timaukel 52 C3
Tinguiririca (Ohi) 29 E6
Tinguiririca (Ohi) 29 E6
Tirúa 32 B6
Titiri (B) 11 G5
Toco 14 D4
Toconao 18 B2
Toconce 15 G4
Toconey 30 C3
Tocopilla 14 B4
Todos Santos (B) 11 F6
Tolar Grande (A) 18 C6
Toledo 22 C2
Tolhuán 24 D6
Tolhuin 53 G5
Toltén 34 C2
Tomasiri (P) 10 A3
Tomé 30 A6
Tongoy 24 D5
Topocalma 28 C5
Torrecilla 30 C6
Torreón 30 B6
Torres del Paine 45 G6
Tortolas 16 D6
Totoral 22 B4
Totoralillo (Ata) 22 D3
Totoralillo (Coq) 24 D4
Totoralillo (Coq) 26 C4

Trafiche 30 C3
Traiguén 32 C5
Traiguén 34 C5
Tranquila 27 F4
Trapi 34 D6
Trapiche 26 D5
Travesía 22 C3
Treguaco 30 B6
Tregualemu (Mau) 30 B4
Tregualemu (Bio) 33 E2
Tres Cruces 25 E2
Tres Esquinas (Mau) 30 C5
Tres Esquinas (Bio) 30 D6
Tres Esquinas (Bio) 32 D1
Tres Pinos 32 B4
Tres Playitas 22 A5
Trevelín (A) 39 H1
Tricao 31 E2
Tricauco 32 D5
Trinidad 34 B5
Trintre 32 C4
Trompetilla 31 G1
Trovolhue 32 B6
Troyo 33 F5
Trumao 34 C6
Trupén 33 E3
Tucapel 33 E3
Tuina 15 G5
Tulahuén 27 E2
Tulor 18 A1
Tumbes 30 A6
Túnel Angostura 29 F4
Túnel de Chacabuco 29 F2
Túnel Las Raíces 33 F6
Túnel Lo Prado 29 E3
Túnel Zapata 29 E3
Tunga 26 D3
Turco (B) 11 G4
Turiza 12 C2
Turquía 32 C2
Turuben 30 C4
Tutuquén 31 E2

Ujina 13 F6
Ulloma (B) 11 G1
Umagata 10 C5
Unicavén 30 C5
Unihue 32 C2
Unión 17 F1
Uribe 16 D3
Ushuaia (A) 53 E6

Vaitea (EI) 19 G2
Valdivia 34 C4
Valdivia de Paine 29 F4
Valle Castor 53 E4
Valle Chacabuco 41 F6
Valle de la Luna (Valley of the Moon) 15 G6
Valle del Encanto 24 D6
Valle Fértil 22 C2
Valle Hermoso (Ata) 22 D4
Valle Hermoso (Val) 26 D6
Valle Huemules 41 H3
Vallenar 22 B6
Valle Nevado 29 G3
Valparaíso 28 D2
Vaquería 47 H6
Varilla 20 C6
Varillas 17 F4
Vega de Arízaro (A) 18 B6
Vegas Blanca 32 C4
Vegas de Chañaral Alto 21 E6
Vegas de Itata 30 B6
Ventisquero de la Colonia 40 D5
Ventisquero Grey 45 E6
Ventisquero Jorge Montt 43 E4
Ventisquero Lucía 43 E4

Ventisquero O'Higgins 43 F6
Ventisquero San Quintín 40 D5
Ventisquero San Rafael 40 D5
Ventisquero Steffen 43 E1
Vichuquén 30 C1
Victoria 32 D5
Vicuña 25 E4
Vilavila 12 D1
Vilches 31 F3
Vilcuya 29 F1
Villa Alegre 30 D4
Villa Alemana 28 D2
Villa Alerce 32 B3
Villa Alhué 29 E5
Villa Amengual 39 F5
Villa Blanca 13 F2
Villa Cerro Castillo 41 G4
Villa Futalaufquen (A) 39 G1
Villa Industrial 10 C3
Villa La Angostura (A) 37 G1
Villa Mascardi (A) 37 H3
Villa Mercedes 33 E3
Villa Nueva (A) 27 H2
Villa O'Higgins 43 G4
Villa Ortega 41 G1
Villa Pituil (A) 27 H3
Villa Prat 30 D2
Villarica 35 E3
Villa Santa Lucía 39 F2
Villa Seca 30 D4
Villa Tehuelches 48 A4
Villa Traful (A) 35 G6
Villa Vanguardia 39 F3
Villavicencio 30 D4
Villucura 33 E3
Viluco 29 F4
Vilumallin (A) 33 H3
Vilupulli 36 C6
Viña del Mar 28 D2
Viña San Pedro 31 E2
Viñedo Miguel Torres 31 E2
Viñita Baja 25 E4
Vista Alegre 24 D1
Visviri 10 D2
Vivanco 34 D6
Vizcachitas 22 B6
Vodudahue 37 F5
Voipir 35 E3
Volcán Aguas Calientes 18 C2
Volcán Antuco 33 F3
Volcán Azufre o Lastarría 21 G2
Volcán Callaqui 33 F5
Volcán Casablanca 37 F1
Volcán Chillán 33 F1
Volcán Choshuenco 35 E4
Volcán Chuquiananta 10 D3
Volcán Cóndor 41 E2
Volcán Corcovado 39 E2
Volcán Descabezado Chico 31 G3
Volcán Descabezado Grande 31 F4
Volcán Domuyo (A) 31 G6
Volcán El Palomo 29 G6
Volcán El Planchón 31 G2
Volcán Guallatiri 11 E5
Volcán Hornopirén 37 F4
Volcán Irruptuncu 13 F6
Volcán Isluga 13 F1
Volcán Jotabeche 23 F3
Volcán Lanín (A) 35 F4
Volcán Lascar 18 B2
Volcán Licancábur 15 H6
Volcán Linzor 15 H4
Volcán Llaima 35 F1
Volcán Llullaillaco 17 H6
Volcán Lonquimay 33 F6
Volcán Maipo 29 H5
Volcán Melimoyú 39 E4
Volcán Michinmahuida 37 F6

Volcán Miño 15 F1
Volcan Nevado 39 E2
Volcán Ojos del Salado 23 H2
Volcán Olca 13 F6
Volcán Ollagüe 15 G2
Volcán Osorno 37 F2
Volcán Parinacota 11 E4
Volcán Peteroa 31 G3
Volcán Putana (B) 15 H5
Volcán Puyehue 35 E6
Volcán Quetrupillán 35 F3
Volcán Quizapu 31 F4
Volcán Rano A-Roi (EI) 19 F2
Volcán Rano Raraku (EI) 19 G2
Volcán Sajama (B) 11 F4
Volcán San Pablo 15 G3
Volcán San Pedro 15 G3
Volcán Socompa 18 A5
Volcán Tacora 10 C3
Volcán Tinguiririca 31 G1
Volcán Tolhuaca 33 F6
Volcán Tupungatito 29 H3
Volcán Villarica 35 E3

Yacal 31 E2
Yaldad 38 C1
Yerbas Buenas 30 D4
Yumbel (Bio) 32 D2
Yumbel (Bio) 32 D2
Yungay 33 E2

Zanja Pique (A) 49 F4
Zapahuira 10 D4
Zapallar (Val) 26 D6
Zapallar (Coq) 27 E4
Zapallar (Bio) 33 E1
Zapar 18 B1
Zapiga 12 C2
Zemita 30 D6
Zora 10 C4

BEACHES
Chanabaya 12 B6
Chipana 14 B2
Guanillos 14 B2
Hornitos 14 B6
Playa Bandurrias 20 C2
Playa Blanca 12 B5
Playa Corazones 10 B5
Playa del Buque Varado (JF) 19 E6
Playa Huáscar 16 C3
Playa Huayquique 12 B4
Playa Larga 19 E6
Playa Peruana 14 B1
Playa Reñaca 28 D1
Playa Sara 20 C2
Tres Playitas 22 A5

CAPES, HEADLANDS & PENINSULAS
Cabo Bascuñán 24 C1
Cabo Cumming (EI) 19 H2
Cabo de Hornos 55 G4
Cabo Espíritu Santo (A) 49 F6
Cabo Expectación 52 C2
Cabo Froward 51 H3
Cabo Jara 16 C3
Cabo Leones 24 C1
Cabo Norte (EI) 19 F1
Cabo Norte (JF) 19 E6
Cabo O'Higgins (EI) 19 H2
Cabo Paquita 14 B3
Cabo Quedal 36 C2
Cabo Roggewein (EI) 19 H2
Cabo Rugged 44 B4
Cabo San Isidro 52 A3
Cabo San Pío (A) 55 H1
Cabo San Sebastián (A) 53 F2

Cabo Sur (El) 19 F3
Cabo Vírgenes (A) 49 F5
Falso Cabo de Hornos 55 F3
Península Antonio Varas 47 F2
Península Avellaneda (A) 45 F4
Península Barros Arana 47 F3
Península Brecknock 51 H5
Península Cloué 54 C1
Península Córdoba 51 F1
Península de Brunswick 51 H2
Península de Taitao 40 C4
Península Duende 40 B3
Península Dumas 55 E1
Península Esmeralda 40 C5
Península Exmouth 44 D1
Península Florida 43 G5
Península Forelius 40 C5
Península Greenough 51 H4
Península Hardy 55 E2
Península Juan Mazia 48 C6
Península Larenas 42 C2
Península Magallanes (A) 45 F4
Península Mejillones 16 C2
Península Muñoz Gamero 47 F4
Península Negra 42 C4
Península Pasteur 55 E2
Península Poike (El) 19 G2
Península Roca 47 F3
Península Rolando 52 A5
Península Rous 54 C2
Península Sisquelan 40 D4
Península Skiring 40 B3
Península Staines 47 E2
Península Swett 42 C3
Península Tres Montes 40 A5
Península Ulloa 51 F2
Península Videau 43 E3
Península Wharton 44 B2
Península Wilcock 44 D5
Península Zach 47 E4
Puna Piedra Lobos 26 C1
Punta Achira 30 B5
Punta Agua Dulce 14 B4
Punta Alala 14 B5
Punta Alcalde 22 A6
Punta Almanao 36 C4
Punta Amolana 26 C3
Punta Amparo 38 D6
Punta Anegada 48 D5
Punta Anegadeiza 32 A6
Punta Angamos 16 C1
Punta Anita 40 C6
Punta Arenas 14 B3
Punta Arenas 30 C2
Punta Argolla 10 B6
Punta Arvejas 32 A6
Punta Auchernó 39 E1
Punta Baja (El) 19 G2
Punta Ballena (Tar) 12 B3
Punta Ballena (Ant) 20 B3
Punta Ballenita 20 B3
Punta Baquedano 10 B5
Punta Baquedano (El) 19 F2
Punta Barrancas 28 C5
Punta Barranco 38 B2
Punta Blanca (Tar) 10 B5
Punta Blanca (Tar) 14 B2
Punta Blanca (Ant) 14 B4
Punta Boique 38 D2
Punta Bonita 36 C6
Punta Botija 16 C5
Punta Boyeruca 28 C6
Punta Burca 30 A6
Punta Bustamante (A) 49 E2
Punta Cabeza de Vaca 22 B1
Punta Cachos 22 B3
Punta Caleta 38 B3

Punta Camarones 12 B1
Punta Camerón 52 C3
Punta Canas 26 D6
Punta Capitanes 36 C2
Punta Carrizal (Ata) 22 A4
Punta Carrizal (Ata) 24 C2
Punta Carrizalillo 20 B4
Punta Catalina 49 F5
Punta Caucaguapi 36 C4
Punta Cavancha 12 B4
Punta Centinela (Ohi) 28 C5
Punta Centinela (Lag) 38 D1
Punta Chaiguaco 38 B1
Punta Chales 32 A6
Punta Chanchán 34 C3
Punta Checo 36 C6
Punta Chileno 14 B2
Punta Chipana 14 B2
Punta Chomache 14 B1
Punta Choros 36 C4
Punta Chucumata 12 B5
Punta Chulao 37 E5
Punta Chumildén 37 E5
Punta Chungungo 34 C4
Punta Cobija 14 B5
Punta Cogomo 38 C2
Punta Coicoi 30 A6
Punta Colorada 12 B4
Punta Coloso 16 C3
Punta Colún 34 B5
Punta Concón 28 D1
Punta Cóndor 36 C1
Punta Conglomerada 42 A5
Punta Coronel 32 B2
Punta Cucagua 38 D2
Punta Cullín 30 A6
Punta Cullinto 32 B1
Punta Curaumilla 28 D2
Punta Dallas 22 B2
Punta de Arenas (A) 53 F1
Punta de las Islas 32 A6
Punta del Roble 38 B2
Punta Diego 40 B6
Punta Dineley 42 A6
Punta Dora 42 A3
Punta Dos Reyes 16 C5
Punta Duao 30 C1
Punta Dungenes 49 F5
Punta El Morrito 26 C4
Punta Esperanza 36 C5
Punta Estaquilla 36 C3
Punta Farellones 24 C5
Punta Freddy (JF) 19 G6
Punta Frödden 22 B1
Punta Galera 34 B5
Punta Gallegos 40 B3
Punta Gallo 28 D2
Punta Gorda 12 B1
Punta Grande 14 B5
Punta Grande 20 C1
Punta Gruesa (Tar) 12 B5
Punta Gruesa (Coq) 26 C2
Punta Guabún 36 C4
Punta Guanaquero 24 D5
Punta Guanillo 14 B2
Punta Guanillo del Sur 14 B5
Punta Horcón 26 C6
Punta Huechucuicui 36 C4
Punta Hueicolla 34 B5
Punta Huemul 46 B1
Punta Huenocoihue 38 B1
Punta Hueso Ballena (JF) 19 H5
Punta Huesos 26 C5
Punta Iglesia 30 B5
Punta Infieles 20 B5
Punta Isla 19 G5
Punta Jaime 40 D2

Punta Jorge 16 C3
Punta Lacho 28 D3
Punta Lagartos 16 C2
Punta Lagunillas 24 D4
Punta Las Ánimas 20 B5
Punta Las Perdices 26 C2
Punta Lautaro 14 B3
Punta Lavapié (Ant) 20 B3
Punta Lavapié (Bio) 32 A2
Punta Leith 44 D3
Punta Lengua de Vaca 24 C5
Punta Ligua 26 D6
Punta Limarí 24 C6
Punta Limarí Norte 24 C6
Punta Llesquehue 34 B6
Punta Lobería (Ant) 16 C1
Punta Lobería (Coq) 26 C4
Punta Lobos 14 B1
Punta Lobos (Ata) 22 A5
Punta Lobos (Coq) 26 C4
Punta Lobos (Ohi) 28 C6
Punta Lomas 22 B3
Punta Madrid 10 B6
Punta Maiquillahue 34 C3
Punta Manuel 32 B6
Punta Mar Brava 24 D2
Punta Media 22 B2
Punta Mela 30 A6
Punta Merino 40 B6
Punta Mirador 38 B1
Punta Mogote Negro 22 A6
Punta Molles 26 C5
Punta Morguilla 32 A4
Punta Morro 22 B2
Punta Negra (JF) 19 E6
Punta Nihue 34 C3
Punta Norte (JF) 19 G5
Punta Norte 38 B3
Punta O'Higgins (JF) 19 G5
Punta Olleta 38 C2
Punta Oriental 55 H2
Punta Pabellón 38 B2
Punta Paloma 10 B5
Punta Patache 12 B6
Punta Patch 20 B6
Punta Peña Blanca 22 A3
Punta Peñablanca 28 D3
Perro Perro 28 C4
Punta Peumo 26 D6
Punta Pichalo 12 B2
Punta Pichicui 26 D6
Punta Piedras 12 B4
Punta Piojo 12 B3
Punta Plata 16 C6
Punta Poroto 24 D3
Punta Posallaves 16 C6
Punta Pringle 40 A5
Punta Puaucho 34 C1
Punta Pucaihuén 39 E2
Punta Pucatrihue 34 B6
Punta Puga 36 C3
Punta Pullay 30 B5
Punta Queniao 36 D4
Punta Quillagua 36 C3
Punta Quillaipe 37 E3
Punta Quintay 28 D2
Punta Ragged 50 D3
Punta Redonda (El) 19 G2
Punta Rescue 40 B4
Punta Rincón 20 C1
Punta Roa (El) 19 F2
Punta Rocura 34 C4
Punta Ronca 34 C3
Punta Roncura 30 C2
Punta Roth 42 A4
Punta Salado 22 B3
Punta Saliente 36 C5
Punta Salinas (JF) 19 H5

Punta San Juan (El) 19 G1
Punta San Pedro 20 B3
Punta Santa María 52 A2
Punta Sierra 26 C2
Punta Sirena 28 C6
Punta Stockes 44 B6
Punta Sunshine 51 G1
Punta Sur 38 B3
Punta Tablaruca 38 B1
Punta Talca (Coq) 26 C1
Punta Talca (San) 28 D3
Punta Talinay 24 C6
Punta Talquilla 26 C1
Punta Taltal 20 C2
Punta Tames 14 B6
Punta Teatinos 24 D4
Punta Tetas 16 C2
Punta Tiques 38 B2
Punta Tirúa 32 B6
Punta Tomás 26 C3
Punta Topocalma 28 C5
Punta Toro 28 C4
Punta Totoral 22 A4
Punta Tres Cruces 36 D4
Punta Truenos (JF) 19 G5
Punta Tucapel 32 A4
Punta Tunquillax (JF) 19 G5
Punta Urcu 14 B3
Punta Ventana 26 C3
Punta Vial 22 B2
Punta Vicente Porras (JF) 19 E6
Punta Villa Señor 24 C6
Punta Villiers 51 G1
Punta Virgen 26 C2
Punta Weather 38 A3
Punta Yatac 38 D2
Punta Yayes 14 B6
Punta Zenteno 20 B6
Punta Zorra 38 B2

ISLANDS
Archipiélago de las Guaitecas 38 C4
Archipiélago de los Chonos
    38 A6-B5
Archipiélago Guayaneco 42 B2
Archipiélago Reina Adelaida 46 D5
Grupe Theo 46 D5
Grupo Camden 51 G6
Grupo Carmela 46 C2
Grupo Desertores 37 E6
Grupo Gómez Carreño 46 D2
Grupo Lobos 46 C2
Grupo Narborough 46 C5
Grupo Solari 46 D1
Isla Aguirre 51 G5
Isla Agustín 46 B1
Isla Alberto Vargas 43 E3
Isla Aldea 42 B5
Isla Alejandro Selkirk 19 E6
Isla Anafur 44 C4
Isla Angamos 42 B6
Isla Angelotti 46 C2
Isla Apiao 36 D6
Isla Arthur 38 B4
Isla Arturo 44 A1
Isla Ascensión 38 C3
Isla Atilio 38 D4
Isla Auchilu 40 C2
Isla Ayautau 42 C2
Isla Barrios 43 E3
Isla Barros Arana 46 D4
Isla Basket 51 H6
Isla Bayly 55 F3
Isla Benjamín 38 C5
Isla Betecoi 38 C4
Isla Blanca 42 B3
Isla Bolados 38 C5
Isla Bordes 46 D4

Cordillera Pinto 47 G4-5
Cordillera Riesco 47 H6
Cordillera Sarmiento de Gamboa 47 E2-3
Cordillera Serrucho 47 G6
Cordillera Vidal 47 H4
Cordón de la Totora (A) 27 G2
Cordón de Puntas Negras 18 C3-4
Cordón Esmeralda 43 G1
Cordón Marchant 39 E4
Cumbres de San Gregorio 48 C5
Llano de la Paciencia 17 H3
Llano de Pajonal 22 B6
Maunga Otu (El) 19 F2
Maunga Pukatikei (El) 19 H2
Maunga Terevaja (El) 19 F1
Maunga Tuutapu (El) 19 F2
Monte Chaltel o Fitz Roy 45 F1
Monte Muela 51 G2
Monte O'Higgins 44 D2
Monte Pissis (A) 23 G4
Monte San Lorenzo o Cochrane 43 G2
Monte San Valentín o San Clemente 41 E5
Monte Tronador (A) 37 G2
Morrito de Chara 13 F6
Morro Mejillones 16 C1
Nevado de Incahuasi 23 H1
Nevado de Longaví 31 E5
Nevado de San Francisco 23 H1
Nevado de Tres Cruces 23 G2
Nevado El Fraile 23 H1
Nevados de Chillán 33 F2-G2
Nevados de Putre 10 D4
Pampa Alona 13 E5
Pampa Amarilla (A) 29 G2-H2
Pampa Arturo Prat 16 D3
Pampa Blanca 12 C6
Pampa Columtucsa 13 E4-F3
Pampa Cruz Verde (P) 10 A3
Pampa de Camarones 10 B6
Pampa de Chaca 10 B5
Pampa de Chiza 12 C1
Pampa del Asador (A) 43 H3
Pampa de las Zorras 12 B6-C6
Pampa del Avestruz 15 F3
Pampa del Indio Muerto 14 D5-6
Pampa de Loncoloan (A) 35 G1-H1
Pampa de los Bayos 21 H5
Pampa del Tamarugal (Tar) 12 C3-D5
Pampa del Tamarugal (Ant) 15 E3-E5
Pampa de Oxaya 10 C5-D5
Pampa de Tana 12 B2
Pampa Elvira 17 F3-G3
Pampa Engañadora 12 C6
Pampa Higualue 35 F5
Pampa Huasco 13 F4
Pampa Miraje 14 B5
Pampa Moctezuma 15 E5
Pampa Perdiz 12 C4
Pampa San Juan 20 D3
Pampa Tres Arroyos (A) 31 G6
Paso Barrancas 31 G5
Paso Catrinao 31 F6
Paso Cerro Colorado 31 F6
Paso Cochamo 37 G3
Paso Codorniz 43 G3
Paso Coihaique 41 H2
Paso Columpios 33 G2
Paso de Barahona 25 G6
Paso de Caririñe 35 F4
Paso de Chollay 25 G2
Paso de Delgado o de la Colorada 27 H3
Paso de Guaitiquina 18 D3
Paso de Icalma 35 G1
Paso de Jama 18 D2

Paso del Agua Negra 25 H5
Paso de la Honda o del Portillo 27 F5
Paso de la Laguna de la Overa (A) 27 F2
Paso de la Laguna Sico 18 D4
Paso del Arco 35 G1
Paso del Bermejo 29 H1
Paso de Llaima o Santa María 35 G2
Paso del Macho 31 F6
Paso de los Piuquenes 27 F3
Paso del Planchón 31 G2
Paso del Rincón de la Flecha 23 E6
Paso del Rubio 27 G6
Paso del Verde 27 F2
Paso de Menéndez 37 F6
Paso de Molina 29 G6
Paso de Pelambres 27 F4
Paso de Peña Negra 23 F5
Paso de Pérez Rosales 37 G2
Paso de Pino Hachado 35 G1
Paso de Pircas Negras 23 F4
Paso de Potrerillos 31 G3
Paso de Pucón Mahuida 33 G4
Paso de San Francisco 23 H1
Paso Desecho 33 G3
Paso El Portillo 31 G5
Paso Huahum 35 F5
Paso Lagunas de Epulafquén 33 G2
Paso Monte Aymond 48 D4
Paso Origen del Río Potrerillos 25 G3
Paso Palena 39 G3
Paso Pehuenche o del Maule 31 G5
Paso Portezuelo Baguales I 45 F5
Paso Portezuelo Baguales IV 45 G5
Paso Rodolfo Roballos 41 G6
Paso Trolón 31 G4
Portezuelo Argentino (A) 29 H3
Portezuelo de Chapiquiña 10 D4
Portezuelo de Japu o Caranguillas 11 E5
Portezuelo de las Lágrimas 29 G6
Portezuelo del Cajón 15 H6
Portezuelo de los Patos o Cuesta Colorada 23 G2
Portezuelo de los Piuquenes 29 H3
Portezuelo del Tupungato 29 H3
Portezuelo de Valle Ancho Norte 23 G3
Portezuelo Huemules 41 H3
Portezuelo Llullaillaco 17 H6
Portezuelo Tambo Quemado 11 E4
Portezuelo Vidal Gormaz 23 F3
Puna (El) 19 F2
Rano Kau (El) 19 F3
Sierra Almeida 17 H4
Sierra Amarilla 16 D6
Sierra Arturo Prat 47 F2
Sierra Banderita 23 E1
Sierra de las Palas 25 G2
Sierra del Cóndor 25 F2
Sierra del Fritis 22 C3-4
Sierra del Jardín 17 F3-4
Sierra del Peñón (A) 23 G5
Sierra del Toro Negro (A) 23 H5
Sierra de Moreno 15 F2
Sierra de Sangra 43 G4-5
Sierra de Setiembre 20 C3
Sierra de Tatulo del Medio 25 G2
Sierra de Valdivieso 52 D5-6
Sierra de Varas 21 F1
Sierra de Vinchina (A) 23 H6
Sierra Dorotea 47 G2
Sierra los Colorados 14 C3-4
Sierra Miranda (Ant) 16 D2
Sierra Miranda (Ata) 21 E4-5

Sierra Morena (P) 10 A4
Sierra Pajonales 22 C1
Sierra Penafiel 17 E6-F6
Sierra Remiendos 16 C5-D5
Sierra Vicuña Mackenna 16 D5-6
Tortolas 16 D6
Túnel Angostura 29 F4
Túnel de Chacabuco 29 F2
Túnel Las Raíces 33 F6
Túnel Lo Prado 29 E3
Túnel Zapata 29 E3
Vaitea (El) 19 G2
Volcán Aguas Calientes 18 C2
Volcán Antuco 33 F3
Volcán Azufre o Lastarría 21 G2
Volcán Callaqui 33 F5
Volcán Casablanca 37 F1
Volcán Chillán 33 F1
Volcán Choshuenco 35 E4
Volcán Chuquiananta 10 D3
Volcán Cóndor 41 E2
Volcán Corcovado 39 E2
Volcán Descabezado Chico 31 G3
Volcán Descabezado Grande 31 F4
Volcán Domuyo (A) 31 G6
Volcán El Palomo 29 G6
Volcán El Planchón 31 G2
Volcán Guallatiri 11 E5
Volcán Hornopirén 37 F4
Volcán Irruptuncu 13 F6
Volcán Isluga 13 F1
Volcán Lanín (A) 35 F4
Volcán Lascar 18 B2
Volcán Licancábur 15 H6
Volcán Linzor 15 H4
Volcán Llaima 35 F1
Volcán Llullaillaco 17 H6
Volcán Lonquimay 33 F6
Volcán Maipo 29 H5
Volcán Melimoyú 39 E4
Volcán Michinmahuida 37 F6
Volcán Miño 15 F1
Volcan Nevado 39 E2
Volcán Ojos del Salado 23 H2
Volcán Olca 19 G2
Volcán Ollagüe 15 G2
Volcán Osorno 37 F2
Volcán Parinacota 11 E4
Volcán Peteroa 31 G3
Volcán Putana (B) 15 H5
Volcán Puyehue 35 E6
Volcán Quetrupillán 35 F3
Volcán Quizapu 31 F4
Volcán Rano A-Roi (El) 19 F2
Volcán Rano Raraku (El) 19 G2
Volcán Sajama (B) 11 F4
Volcán San Pablo 15 G3
Volcán San Pedro 15 G3
Volcán Socompa 18 A5
Volcán Tacora 10 C3
Volcán Tinguiririca 31 G1
Volcán Tolhuaca 33 F6
Volcán Tupungatito 29 H3
Volcán Villarica 35 E3

NATIONAL PARKS
Área de Protección Radal Siete Tazas 31 F4
Monumento Natural Alerce Costero 34 B5
Monumento Natural Contulmo 32 B5
Monumento Natural Cueva del Milodón 47 G2
Monumento Natural Dos Lagunas 41 G2
Monumento Natural Laguna de los Cisnes 52 B1

Monumento Natural La Portada 16 C3
Monumento Natural Los Pingüinos 48 B6
Monumento Natural Pichasca 25 E5
Monumento Natural Salar de Surire 11 E6
Parque Nacional Alberto de Agostini 52 B5
Parque Nacional Alerce Andino 37 F3
Parque Nacional Archipiélago de Juan Fernández 19 F5
Parque Nacional Bernardo O'Higgins 42 D4
Parque Nacional Cabo de Hornos 55 G3
Parque Nacional Chiloé 36 C5
Parque Nacional Conguillío 35 F1
Parque Nacional El Morado 29 G4
Parque Nacional Francisco Perito Moreno (A) 43 G3
Parque Nacional Fray Jorge 24 C6
Parque Nacional Hornopirén 37 F4
Parque Nacional Huerquehue 35 F2
Parque Nacional Isla Guamblín 38 A6
Parque Nacional Isla Magdalena 39 E5
Parque Nacional Isluga 13 E2
Parque Nacional La Campana 29 E2
Parque Nacional Lago Palena 39 G3
Parque Nacional Laguna del Laja 33 F3
Parque Nacional Laguna San Rafael 40 B5
Parque Nacional Lanin (A) 35 G4
Parque Nacional Lauca 10 D5
Parque Nacional Llanos de Challe 22 A5
Parque Nacional Los Alerces (A) 37 G6
Parque Nacional Los Glaciares (A) 45 F3
Parque Nacional Los Guaitecas 40 C3
Parque Nacional Nahuelbuta 32 C4
Parque Nacional Nevado de Tres Cruces 23 G1
Parque Nacional Pali Aike 48 D4
Parque Nacional Pan de Azúcar 20 B4
Parque Nacional Puyehue 37 F1
Parque Nacional Queulat 39 F5
Parque Nacional Rapa Nui (El) 19 G2
Parque Nacional Río Simpson 41 G2
Parque Nacional Tolhuaca 33 E5
Parque Nacional Torres del Paine 45 F6
Parque Nacional Vicente Pérez Rosales 37 F2
Parque Natural Vilches 31 F3
Parque Natural Villarica 35 F3
Parque Natural Pumalin 37 E6
Parque Provincial Aconcagua 29 (A) H1
Parque Provincial Volcán Tupungato (A) 29 H2
Pingüinera Seno Otway 48 A6
Reserva Forestal Alacalufes 46 C4
Reserva Nacional Alacalufes 50 C1
Reserva Nacional Cerro Castillo 41 G3
Reserva Nacional Coihaique 41 G2
Reserva Nacional El Paposo 16 C6

Reserva Nacional Federico Albert 30 B4
Reserva Nacional Isla Mocha 32 A6
Reserva Nacional Katalalixar 42 B4, C2
Reserva Nacional La Chimba 16 C3
Reserva Nacional Lago Cochrane 41 F6
Reserva Nacional Lago Jeinimeni 41 H5
Reserva Nacional Lago Rosselot 39 F4
Reserva Nacional Laguna Peñuelas 28 D2
Reserva Nacional Laguna Torca 30 C1
Reserva Nacional Laguna Varillar 51 H2
Reserva Nacional Las Chinchillas 26 D3
Reserva Nacional Las Vicuñas 11 E5
Reserva Nacional Los Flamencos 18 A1
Reserva Nacional Los Ruiles 30 B4
Reserva Nacional Magallanes 51 H1
Reserva Nacional Pampa del Tamarugal 12 C3
Reserva Nacional Pampa del Tamarugal 12 C5
Reserva Nacional Pingüino de Humboldt 24 C2
Reserva Nacional Río Clarillo 29 F4
Reserva Nacional Río Los Cipreses 29 F6
Santuario de la Naturaleza Yerba Loca 29 G2
Santuario El Cañi 35 F2

RAILWAY STATIONS
Adolfo Zaldivar 17 G4
Agua Buena 16 D5
Aguas Blancas 17 E4
Allipén 34 D2
Ancagual 34 D3
Auco 26 D3
Balmaceda 20 D1
Barriles 14 B4
Bilbao 32 D6
Buena Esperanza 22 B6
Calafquén 35 E3
Candelaria 32 D3
Cardonal 28 C6
Caserón 22 C2
Casma 36 D2
Central 12 C5
Cerillos 24 D4
Cerritos Bayos 15 E6
Cerro Gordo 12 D6
Chacance 14 D5
Chacayal 34 C6
Chacritas 22 B5
Champulli 34 D6
Chañar 25 E2
Chanchan 32 B4
Charrúa 32 D2
Chulo 22 D2
Comodoro Py (A) 48 A3
Conchi 15 F4
Cuñibal 32 D3
El Desierto 17 E3
El Manzano 35 E1
El Natre 34 D1
El Romero 22 B6
Escuadrón 32 B2
Esmeralda 28 D3

Estación El Toco 14 D4
Gualcuna 25 E3
Guzmán 34 D6
Hermanos Clark 29 G1
Huinganes 30 C3
Ingeniero Barriga 26 D4
Ingeniero Capps (A) 48 B3
Inspector Fernández 32 D5
Lacalle 17 E5
La Cumbre 29 F1
Lambert 24 D4
Lanalhue 32 B4
Larrain Alcalde 28 C6
Las Cañas 26 D4
Las Viñas 32 D4
Lata 16 D3
Latorre 16 D2
Leyda 28 D3
Lipingue 34 D4
Llampos 22 D2
Llano Blanco 33 E4
Llanos 17 E3
Loma Colorada 32 B2
Los Dones 14 C6
Los Vientos 17 E6
Malvilla 28 D3
Margarita 22 C2
Mariquina 34 D3
Martínez de Rosas 34 D2
Mataquito 30 D2
Mauce 28 D1
Melefquén 35 E3
Metrenco 34 D1
Monturaqui 17 H5
Nahuelbuta 32 B5
Ñancul 35 E3
Neurara 17 H4
O'Higgins 16 D3
Ojeda 14 C4
Palermo 32 D3
Palestina 17 E3
Palos Quemados 26 D6
Pampa Ossa 10 C4
Pan de Azúcar 17 H4
Pidima 32 D5
Piedra Colgada 22 C2
Pissis 30 B6
Polapi 15 G3
Polonia 29 E6
Prat 34 D1
Puangue 28 D3
Punta Colorada 25 E2
Punta de Días 22 C4
Purey 34 D4
Quebrada del Agua (A) 18 A6
Quillaico 34 D5
Quillén 32 D6
Ranguelmo 30 B6
Ranquilco 34 C1
Ritoque 28 D1
Roblería 32 D4
San Antonio 12 C5
San Juan 20 D3
Santa Fe 14 D3
Santa Rosa 12 C4
Sarmiento 31 E1
Socompa 17 H5
Tinguiririca 29 E6
Toledo 22 C2
Turquía 32 C2
Tutuquén 31 E2
Unihue 32 C2
Uribe 16 D3
Valle Fértil 22 C2
Varillas 17 F4
Vilcuya 29 F1
Viluco 29 F4
Yumbel 32 D2

RIVERS, BAYS & LAKES
Arroyo Potrerillo (A) 27 H3
Bahía Adventure 38 B6
Bahía Agua Fresca 52 A2
Bahía Anna Pink 40 B3
Bahía Asasao 38 C2
Bahía Barrister 50 C1
Bahía Beaufort 47 E6
Bahía Bossi 44 B3
Bahía Breaker 51 E3
Bahía Brookes 52 C5
Bahía Carrizal 24 C2
Bahía Chanco 30 B4
Bahía Chiquinata 12 B4
Bahía Chomache 34 B1
Bahía Choros 24 D2
Bahía Cobquecura 30 B5
Bahía Cocotué 36 C4
Bahía Coliumo 30 A6
Bahía Conchali 26 C4
Bahía Cook 54 B1
Bahía Copiapó 22 B2
Bahía Coquimbo 24 D4
Bahía Cucao 36 B6
Bahía Cumberland (JF) 19 H5
Bahía Darwin 40 B2
Bahía de Caldera 22 B1
Bahía de Carnero 32 A3
Bahía de la Colonia (JF) 19 E6
Bahía de Laguna Verde 28 D2
Bahía de La Perouse (EI) 19 G1
Bahía del Sur 55 E3
Bahía de Mejillones del Sur 16 C1
Bahía de San Pedro 36 C1
Bahía Dineley 42 A6
Bahía Expectación 44 C4
Bahía Felipe 48 C6
Bahía Filton 52 B5
Bahía Gallegos (A) 49 E2
Bahía Gente Grande 48 C6
Bahía Guanaqueros 24 D5
Bahía Harvey 42 B2
Bahía Herradura de Guayacán 24 D4
Bahía Ibáñez 41 G4
Bahía Inglesa 22 B1
Bahía Inútil 52 C2
Bahía Isla Blanca 20 B2
Bahía La Cañas 30 B3
Bahía La Vaquería (JF) 19 H5
Bahía Lee 48 C6
Bahía Linao 36 D4
Bahía Lomas 49 E5
Bahía Maiquillahue 34 C3
Bahía Manao 36 D4
Bahía Maullín 36 C3
Bahía Moreno 16 C2
Bahía Nassau 55 F2
Bahía Nuestra Señora 20 C2
Bahía Oglander 55 H2
Bahía Otway 50 D2
Bahía Parker 46 D5
Bahía Porvenir 52 B2
Bahía Posesión 49 E4
Bahía Queule 34 C3
Bahía Salado 22 B3
Bahía Salvación 44 B6
Bahía San Andrés 40 A5
Bahía San Francisco 55 G4
Bahía San Quintín 40 C5
Bahía San Sebastián (A) 53 E1
Bahía Santiago 48 D5
Bahía Spartan 44 A3
Bahía Stewart (Ais) 40 A4
Bahía Stewart (Mag) 51 H6
Bahía Stokes 51 F4
Bahía Tarn 42 C2
Bahía Teniente 26 C1
Bahía Tic Toc 39 E3

Bahía Tierras Blancas (JF) 19 G5
Bahía Tongoy 24 C5
Bahía Totoralillo 20 B6
Bahía Tribune 42 C5
Bahía Whitesand 48 B6
Bahía Windhond 55 F2
Bahía Wodsworth 47 E6
Boca de Canales 42 C2
Boca del Guafo 38 B3
Brazo Chacabuco 43 G6
Brazo Noreste 43 G5
Brazo Noroeste 43 F5
Brazo Norte (A) 45 F4
Brazo Oeste 43 F5
Brazo Sur (A) 45 F5
Brazo Sur del Río Coig (A) 48 A2
Cajón Troncoso 31 F5
Caleta Agua Dulce 16 C4
Caleta Agua Salada 16 C4
Caleta Anakena (EI) 19 G1
Caleta Andrade 41 E1
Caleta Apolillado 24 C2
Caleta Arrayán 24 D3
Caleta Ayacara 37 E5
Caleta Bandurria del Sur 16 C2
Caleta Barco 28 D2
Caleta Barquito 20 B5
Caleta Barranquillas 22 B3
Caleta Blanco Encalada 16 C5
Caleta Bolfín 16 C3
Caleta Buena 12 B3
Caleta Caramucho 12 B6
Caleta Chacaya 14 B6
Caleta Chaihuin 34 B4
Caleta Chañaral 24 C1
Caleta Chica 12 B2
Caleta Chipana 14 B2
Caleta Chucumata 12 B5
Caleta Cifuncho 20 B3
Caleta Colorada 16 C6
Caleta Coloso 16 C3
Caleta Cóndor 36 C1
Caleta de Camarones 12 B1
Caleta de Gatico 14 B5
Caleta El Cobre 16 C5
Caleta El Pedregal 20 B5
Caleta Esmeralda 20 B4
Caleta Esperanza 52 C2
Caleta Flamenco 20 B6
Caleta Gualaguala 14 B6
Caleta Guanillo del Norte 14 B2
Caleta Guanillo del Sur 14 B5
Caleta Guayasca 36 C1
Caleta Hanga Oteo (EI) 19 F1
Caleta Herradura de Mejillones 16 C1
Caleta Horcón 26 D6
Caleta Hotuiti (EI) 19 G2
Caleta Junín 12 B2
Caleta Lacao 26 C2
Caleta La Ligua 26 D5
Caleta Lameguapi 34 B5
Caleta Las Docas 28 D2
Caleta La Serena 30 B4
Caleta Lautaro 14 B2
Caleta Loa 14 B2
Caleta Los Hornos 24 D3
Caleta Maicolpué 34 B6
Caleta Maitencillo de Coquimbo 26 C2
Caleta Mala 26 C3
Caleta Mansa 34 B6
Caleta Mataura 46 C6
Caleta Mejillones del Norte 12 B3
Caleta Michilla 14 B6
Caleta Milagro 34 B5
Caleta Molles 26 D5
Caleta Morritos Norte 26 C2

Caleta Navidad 28 C4
Caleta Obispito 20 B6
Caleta Obispo 20 B6
Caleta Oscuro 26 C3
Caleta Pabellón de Pica 12 B6
Caleta Pajonal 22 B3
Caleta Pan de Azúcar 20 B4
Caleta Pisagua Viejo 12 B2
Caleta Playa Tontado 22 A6
Caleta Punta Arenas 14 B3
Caleta Quidico 32 B5
Caleta Río Seco 14 B1
Caleta Tames 14 B6
Caleta Tirúa 32 B6
Caleta Totoral Bajo 22 A4
Caleta Totaral de Lengua de Vaca
    24 C5
Caleta Totoralillo 24 D3
Caleta Tragagente 16 C5
Caleta Tumán 28 C5
Caleta Vitor 10 B5
Caleta Zenteno 20 B6
Canal Abra 51 E2
Canal Adalberto 42 C5
Canal Albatros 42 B4
Canal Andrés 44 C4
Canal Apiao 36 D6
Canal Baker 43 E4
Canal Ballenero 52 A6
Canal Bárbara 51 G4
Canal Barbarrosa 42 B3
Canal Beagle 55 G1
Canal Castillo 42 A5
Canal Castro 46 C2
Canal Cheap 40 B6-C6
Canal Cockburn 51 G5
Canal Concepción 44 C5
Canal Costa 40 D2
Canal Cutler 46 D3
Canal Darwin 40 C2
Canal de Chacao 36 C4
Canal de los Témpanos (A) 45 F4
Canal Desertores 37 E6
Canal Errázuriz 40 D2
Canal Esmeralda 46 C5
Canal Esteban 44 D6
Canal Euston 47 G5
Canal Fallos 42 B4
Canal Farquhar 42 D5
Canal Ignacio 44 B6
Canal King 38 C5
Canal Ladrillero 44 B1
Canal Magdalena 52 A4
Canal Mesier 42 C3
Canal Miramar 44 A2
Canal Moraleda 38 D5
Canal Murray 55 E1
Canal Octubre 42 A4
Canal Oeste 44 B5
Canal Picton 44 B2
Canal Pitt 44 D5
Canal Puyuguapi 39 E6
Canal Romanche 55 E3
Canal Sarmiento de Gamboa 46 D2
Canal Smith 46 D3-D6
Canal Trinidad 44 B3
Canal Troya 43 E3
Canal Uribe 46 C3
Canal Valdés 47 F3
Canal Whiteside 52 B3
Canal Wide 44 D3
Chorrillo Solitario (A) 48 B2
El Manzano 48 A5
Embalse Bullileo 31 E5
Embalse Cogotí 27 E2
Embalse de Caritaya 10 D6
Embalse Digua 30 D5
Embalse El Yeso 29 G4

Embalse Huechún 29 F2
Embalse Las Paloma 25 E6
Embalse Machicura 31 E4
Embalse Rapel 28 D5
Embalse Recoleta 25 E5
Ensenada Chaitén 39 E1
Ensenada Mar Gruesa 24 C6
Ensenada San Blas 46 B2
Ensenada Toltén (JF) 19 E6
Ensenada Totoralillo 26 C5
Estero Alhué 29 E4
Estero Alicahue 27 E5
Estero Antivero 29 F6
Estero Camisas 27 E4
Estero Casablanca 28 D2
Estero Chimparongo 31 E1
Estero Codegua 29 F5
Estero de Chocalán 29 E4
Estero de Nilahue 28 C6
Estero de Puangue 29 E3
Estero de Quinahue 30 D1
Estero de Upeo 31 F2
Estero de Yali 28 D4
Estero Falcón 44 D2
Estero Gulrvilo 28 D6
Estero Las Palmas 27 E5
Estero Lolol 28 D6
Estero los Puercos 30 D3
Estero Millahue 26 D3
Estero Punitaqui 26 D1
Estero Pupio 26 D4
Estero Quitralco 41 E3
Estero Reloncaví 37 F3
Estero Rosario 28 C5
Estero San Miguel 28 C6
Estero Temuco 33 E2
Estero Tircahue 31 E3
Estero Topocalma 28 C5
Estero Valle Hermoso 27 E2
Estero Vichuquén 30 C1
Estrecho de Magallanes 47 E6
Estrecho Nelson 46 B2
Estuario Silva Palma 51 G1
Fiordo Alejandro 40 B4
Fiordo Asia 45 E5
Fiordo Burns 40 B3
Fiordo Comau o Leptepu 37 F5
Fiordo Cornish 40 B4
Fiordo Cupquelán 41 E4
Fiordo Elefantes 40 D4
Fiordo Hoppner 40 A5
Fiordo Largo 37 F6
Fiordo Newman 40 B5
Fiordo Peel 44 D6
Fiordo San Esteban 40 B4
Fiordo Steffen 43 E2
Golfo Almirante Montt 47 F3
Golfo Corcovado 38 D1-2
Golfo Coronados 36 C3
Golfo de Ancud 37 E4
Golfo de Arauco 32 B2
Golfo de Penas 40 B6
Golfo Ladrillero 44 A1
Golfo San Esteban 40 C6
Golfo Sarmiento de Gamboa 46 B4
Golfo Tres Montes 40 B5
Golfo Trinidad 44 A3
Golfo Xaultegua 51 E1
Hanga Vinapu (EI) 19 F3
Lago Abascal 37 F5
Lago Alegre 43 G3
Lago Aluminé (A) 35 G2
Lago Amalia (A) 53 E3
Lago Amutui Quimei (A) 39 G1
Lago Anibal Pinto 47 G3
Lago Antuk (A) 53 G5
Lago Argentino (A) 45 G4
Lago Azul 37 G4

Lago Balmaceda 47 G3
Lago Bayo 41 E4
Lago Belgrano (A) 43 H3
Lago Bello 52 D1
Lago Bertrand 41 F6
Lago Blanco (A) 41 H3
Lago Blanco 52 D4
Lago Bórquez 43 E4
Lago Briceño 43 G4
Lago Bruch 47 F1
Lago Buenos Aires (A) 41 H4
Lago Burmeister (A) 43 H3
Lago Cabral (A) 43 H6
Lago Caburga 35 F2
Lago Calafquén 35 E3
Lago Caro 41 F3
Lago Castor 41 G2
Lago Cayutué 37 F2
Lago de Chacabuco 43 G1
Lago Chaiguaco 38 C1
Lago Chaiguata 38 C2
Lago Chapo 37 F3
Lago Cheepelmuth (A) 53 G5
Lago Chico 52 D4
Lago Cholila (A) 37 G5
Lago Christie 43 G3
Lago Chungará 11 E4
Lago Claro 41 E2
Lago Cochrane 41 G6
Lago Colico 35 E2
Lago Cóndor 41 E2
Lago Conguillío 35 F1
Lago Constancia 35 F6
Lago Copa 39 E6
Lago Correntoso (A) 35 F6
Lago Coyte (A) 41 H1
Lago Cronómetro 39 H2
Lago Cucao 36 C6
Lago Currahué (A) 35 F4
Lago de Coipasa (B) 13 H1
Lago de Grey 45 F6
Lago de las Rocas 37 G4
Lago de las Torres 39 F6
Lago de los Palos 41 F1
Lago del Sello (A) 41 H6
Lago del Toro 47 F1
Lago de Natri 36 C6
Lago Deseada 52 B1
Lago Deseado 53 E5
Lago Diana 47 G3
Lago Dickson 45 F6
Lago Dulcinea (A) 45 H6
Lago Elena 40 B4
Lago Elizalde 41 F2
Lago Ellis 41 E2
Lago Epuyén (A) 37 H5
Lago Escondido 39 E6
Lago Esmeralda 43 G1
Lago Espolón 39 F2
Lago Esquel (A) 39 H1
Lago Fagnano (Kami) (A) 53 F5
Lago Falkner (A) 35 F6
Lago Fontana (A) 39 G6
Lago Fuego (A) 53 G4
Lago Futalaufquen (A) 37 G6
Lago Galletué 35 G1
Lago General Carrera 41 F5
Lago General Vintter (A) 39 G4
Lago Grande (A) 45 H4
Lago Gris 35 F6
Lago Guillelmo (A) 37 H3
Lago Gutiérrez (A) 37 H2
Lago Hermoso (A) 35 F6
Lago Huechulafquen (A) 35 G4
Lago Huelpilún 35 E2
Lago Huillinco 36 C6
Lago Huishue 35 E6
Lago Icalma 35 G1

Lago Interior 37 F6
Lago Jeinement 41 G5
Lago J. Roca (A) 37 G3
Lago Kruger (A) 37 G6
Lago Lácar (A) 35 F5
Lago La Paloma 41 G3
Lago La Plata 39 F6
Lago Lapparent 41 G4
Lago Largo 41 G1
Lago Llanquihue 37 E2
Lago Lleulleu 32 B5
Lago Lolog (A) 35 F5
Lago Lynch 52 D4
Lago Maihue 35 E5
Lago Martín (A) 37 G3
Lago Mascardi (A) 37 G2
Lago Meliquina (A) 35 G6
Lago Menéndez (A) 37 G6
Lago Mercedes 53 E3
Lago Meullin 41 E1
Lago Nahuel Huapi (A) 37 H2
Lago Nansen (A) 43 H3
Lago Navarino 55 G1
Lago Neltume 35 E4
Lago Nordenskjöld 45 F6
Lago O'Higgins 43 F5
Lago Paguipulli 35 E4
Lago Palena 39 G3
Lago Palique (A) 45 H6
Lago Pampa Alta 41 H1
Lago Peilaifa 35 F3
Lago Pirihueico 35 F4
Lago Pollux 41 G2
Lago Portales 41 F2
Lago Porteño 47 F1
Lago Posadas (A) 43 H2
Lago Presidente Rios 40 C4
Lago Presidente Roosevelt 39 F6
Lago Puelo (A) 37 G5
Lago Pueyrredón (A) 43 H1
Lago Puyehue 35 E6
Lago Quetru 43 F3
Lago Quillén (A) 35 G3
Lago Ranco 34 D5
Lago Reñihue 37 F6
Lago Riesco 41 F2
Lago Riñihue 35 E4
Lago Risopatrón 39 E4
Lago Rivadavia (A) 37 G6
Lago Roca (A) 45 F5
Lago Rosario 39 H2
Lago Rosselot 39 F4
Lago Rupanco 37 E1
Lago San Antonio 38 C1
Lago San Martín (A) 43 G6
Lago Sarmiento (A) 45 H5
Lago Sarmiento 45 F6
Lagos de la Pascua (A) 53 E2
Lago Situación (A) 39 G1
Lago Sofía 47 G2
Lago Steffen (A) 37 G3
Lago Tagua Tagua 37 F3
Lago Tannhauser (A) 45 F3
Lago Tar (A) 43 H6
Lago Tarahuin 36 C6, 38 C1
Lago Tepuhueco 36 C6
Lago Todos Los Santos 37 F2
Lago Traful (A) 35 G6
Lago Trinidad 34 B5
Lago Tromen (A) 35 G3
Lago Tyndall 47 F1
Lago Verde (A) 41 H4
Lago Verde 39 F4
Lago Vichuquén 30 C1
Lago Viedma (A) 45 F2-H2
Lago Villarica 35 E2
Lago Windhond 55 F2
Lago Yehuin (A) 53 F5

Lago Yelcho 39 F2
Lago Yulton 39 E6
Lago Zenteno 41 F2
Laguna Agrio (A) 33 G5
Laguna Amarga 45 F6
Laguna Aricota (P) 10 A1
Laguna Azul 45 F6
Laguna Barco 33 G5
Laguna Bismarck (A) 48 D3
Laguna Blanca (Tar) 10 D2
Laguna Blanca (Mag) 48 A5
Laguna Brava (A) 23 G5
Laguna Budi 34 C1
Laguna Cabeza del Mar 48 B6
Laguna Cari Lauquen (A) 31 G6
Laguna Casimiro 48 B5
Laguna Cauquenes 29 F5
Laguna Chaxa 18 A2
Laguna Colbún 31 E4
Laguna Colorado (A) 48 B3
Laguna Colorado (B) 15 H4
Laguna Cóndor (A) 47 H3
Laguna Cotacotani 11 E4
Laguna de Aculeo 29 E4
Laguna de Batuco 29 F2
Laguna de Colorados (A) 21 H4
Laguna de la Azufrera 21 G1
Laguna de la Invernada 31 F4
Laguna de la Laja 33 G2
Laguna del Inca 29 G1
Laguna del Maule 31 G5
Laguna del Negro Francisco 23 F3
Laguna de Los Cisnes 52 B1
Laguna de los Patos (A) 21 H3
Laguna del Toro 48 A4-5
Laguna de Matanzas 28 D4
Laguna de Pescado (A) 53 G5
Laguna Dial 31 F6
Laguna Diamante (A) 29 H5
Laguna Ema 52 D2
Laguna Escondida 21 G6
Laguna Esperanza (A) 47 H1
Laguna Fea (A) 31 G5
Laguna Isola Bella (A) 48 C2
Laguna La Leona (A) 48 D2
Laguna Lanalhue 32 B5
Laguna Larga 48 B4
Laguna Larga (A) 47 H3
Laguna La Rubia (A) 45 H2
Laguna Lejía 18 B3
Laguna Malleco 33 E5
Laguna Miñiques 18 B3
Laguna Miscanti 18 B3
Laguna Mucalliri (B) 13 G2
Laguna Negra (A) 31 G5
Laguna Negra 29 H5
Laguna Pali Aike (A) 48 C3
Laguna Parinacota 13 E1
Laguna Pastos Grandes (B) 15 H3
Laguna Peñuelas 28 D2
Laguna Potrok Aike (A) 48 C3
Laguna Quepe 33 E6
Laguna Riesco 47 G6
Laguna Salada (A) 48 B1
Laguna San Rafael 40 D5
Laguna Santa Rosa 23 F1
Lagunas Bravas 21 G5
Lagunas de Epulafquén (A) 33 G1
Lagunas de Morro Gay (A) 48 A3
Lagunas de Teno 31 G2
Laguna Seca (A) 49 E2
Laguna Serrano 52 B1
Laguna Talar 18 B4
Laguna Tapo Aike (A) 45 H6
Laguna Tara 18 D1
Laguna Torca 30 C1
Laguna Travesía (A) 47 H1
Laguna Tuyajto 18 C4

Laguna Varvarco Campos (A) 31 F6
Laguna Verde (A) 23 G3
Laguna Verde (B) 15 H6
Laguna Verde (Ata) 23 G3
Laguna Verde (Ara) 35 F1
Laguna Verde (Mag) 52 B1
Laguna Vergara 52 D1
Laguna Villacota (P) 10 B1
Paso Aviador Ibáñez 51 F5
Paso Boquerón 52 B2
Paso del Indio 44 C1
Paso del Medio 40 D2
Paso Goree 55 G2
Paso Inglés 51 G3
Paso Nuevo 52 B1
Paso Picton 55 G1
Paso Richmond 55 H2
Paso Suroeste 42 B3
Paso Tarleton 46 D2
Paso Wakefield 51 E4
Primera Angostura 48 D5
Puerto Pichidangui 26 C5
Quebrada Agua Blanca (A) 25 H5
Quebrada Algarrobal 22 C5
Quebrada Ateleura 26 D3
Quebrada Carrizal 22 B4
Quebrada Carrizalillo 22 B5
Quebrada Carrizalillo 22 D3
Quebrada de Aguas Blancas 18 B2
Quebrada de Anchuña 20 C2
Quebrada de Apanza 10 C6
Quebrada de Arcas 15 E3
Quebrada de Aroma 12 D3
Quebrada de Aroma 13 E2
Quebrada de Azapa 10 C5
Quebrada de Cobani (P) 10 C3
Quebrada de Camiña o de Tana
   12 C2
Quebrada de Carrizo 21 E4
Quebrada de Cascabeles 20 C2
Quebrada de Caunani (P) 10 C3
Quebrada de Chanchoquín 22 D6
Quebrada de Chiza 12 B1
Quebrada de Comaronea 24 D5
Quebrada de Coscaya 13 E3
Quebrada de Curijmalla 10 D6
Quebrada de Escritos (P) 10 B4
Quebrada de Falca (P) 10 B3
Quebrada de Gallinazos o de Con-
   cordia (P) 10 B4
Quebrada de Garza o Calisama
   10 C6
Quebrada de Guamanga 20 C6
Quebrada de Guanaqueros 17 H5
Quebrada de Guatacondo 13 E6
Quebrada de Hospicio (P) 10 B4
Quebrada de Juncal 20 D4
Quebrada de la Cachina 20 D3
Quebrada de la Higuera 10 C5
Quebrada de Laquillas 21 F2
Quebrada de la Ramada 13 E6
Quebrada del Boquerón 22 B4
Quebrada del Calvario 25 F3
Quebrada del Chaco 21 E2
Quebrada de los Horcones 29 H1
Quebrada del Patón 23 F2
Quebrada del Salado 20 C5
Quebrada del Totoral 22 B4
Quebrada de Matancilla 20 C1
Quebrada de Mejillones 16 D1
Quebrada de Miñimiñi 12 C1
Quebrada de Pachingo 24 C5
Quebrada de Paipote 23 F2
Quebrada de Pastos Largos 21 F6
Quebrada de Putre 10 D4
Quebrada de Quisma 13 E5
Quebrada de Retamilla 12 C2
Quebrada de San Miguel 22 D2

Quebrada de Seca 13 E4
Quebrada de Sichal 15 E2
Quebrada de Soga 12 D2
Quebrada de Sotoca 12 D2
Quebrada de Suca o de Nama
   12 C1
Quebrada de Taltal 20 D2
Quebrada de Tambillo 13 E4
Quebrada de Tarapacá 13 E3
Quebrada de Tocomar 17 G6
Quebrada de Tuina 15 F5
Quebrada de Umallani 10 C6
Quebrada de Vitor 10 C6
Quebrada Doña Inés Chica 20 D4
Quebrada El Peralillo 20 C5
Quebrada El Tabaco 25 F2
Quebrada Espíritu Santo 26 D2
Quebrada Higuerani (P) 10 C3
Quebrada Honda 24 A6
Quebrada Honda 24 D3
Quebrada Las Barrancas 24 D3
Quebrada las Chacras 25 E3
Quebrada Las Llosyas 10 B5
Quebrada Olivares (A) 25 G6
Quebrada Pachuy 25 G2
Quebrada Pan de Azúcar 20 C4
Quebrada Salitrosa o Flamenco
   20 C6
Quebrada San Andrés 23 E1
Quebrada San Juan 22 A6
Quebrada Seca 25 E6
Quebrada Tignamar 10 D5
Quebrada Tongoicillo 24 D5
Quebrada Vitor 10 B5
Rada Chigualoco 26 C4
Rada Curanipe 30 B4
Rada de Buchupureo 30 B5
Rada de Paposo 20 C1
Rada el Algarrobo 28 D2
Rada Llico 30 C1
Río Abtao 36 C5
Río Agrio (A) 33 H4
Río Agua Negra (A) 25 H5
Río Aluminé (A) 35 G2
Río Ancoa 31 E4
Río Ansilta (A) 27 H3
Río Arenisca (A) 43 H5
Río Atuel (A) 31 H1
Río Atutia (A) 27 G1
Río Baker 41 F6
Río Barros (B) 11 H6
Río Biobío (Bio) 32 C3, 32 D4
Río Biobío (Ara) 33 F6
Río Blanco (A) 23 F5
Río Blanco (A) 27 G4
Río Blanco (A) 29 H6
Río Blanco (Ohi) 29 G5
Río Blanco (Mau) 31 E5
Río Blanco o San Francisco (A)
   25 G6
Río Bote (A) 45 H4
Río Bravo 43 F3
Río Bueno 34 B5
Río Bulelco 32 B3
Río Burco 33 E4
Río Butalcura 36 C5
Río Cachitos 23 F4
Río Calingasta (A) 27 H3
Río Caloboro 32 D3
Río Camarones 10 C4
Río Cañón 41 F1
Río Capahuira (B) 11 G4
Río Caplina (P) 10 B3
Río Caracoles (A) 43 G5
Río Carampangue 32 B3
Río Caranguillas (B) 11 G3
Río Cariquima 13 F2
Río Carrenleufú (A) 39 H3

Río Catanlil (A) 35 H4
Río Cato 33 F1
Río Caunahue 35 E5
Río Cautín 32 D6, 34 C1
Río Cerrado (A) 27 H2
Río Chacabuco 41 F6
Río Chacapoal 29 G5
Río Chacay 25 E6
Río Chaichahuen 34 D6
Río Chaihuin 34 B5
Río Chalinga 27 E3
Río Changaral 30 C6
Río Changomoco (B) 11 F4
Río Chaopa 27 E4
Río Chico 52 D2
Río Chillán 33 F1
Río China Creek 52 D1
Río Chirri 34 D6
Río Cholchol 32 C6
Río Cholguaco 36 C1
Río Cholguán 33 F2
Río Chovellén 30 B4
Río Chubut (A) 37 H5
Río Cisnes 39 F5
Río Clarillo 29 F5
Río Clarillo 29 F6
Río Claro 29 E6
Río Claro 31 E3
Río Claro 31 F1
Río Claro 31 F2
Río Claro 31 F4
Río Claro o Derecho 25 F5
Río Claro Solar 39 F4
Río Cogotí 27 E2
Río Coig (A) 48 D2
Río Coihueco 37 E1
Río Collacagua 13 F4
Río Collón Curá (A) 35 H5
Río Colorado (A) 23 H6
Río Colorado 27 F6
Río Colorado 29 G3
Río Colorado 31 F3
Río Coluco 36 C5
Río Combarbalá 27 E2
Río Cóndor (A) 45 F2
Río Cóndor 52 C4
Río Contaco 34 B6
Río Copiapó 22 B2-D3
Río Copihuelpi 35 E3
Río Cortaderal 29 G6
Río Cosapa (B) 11 G5
Río Cruces 34 C4
Río Cuanaco (A) 45 G3
Río Culleloo 32 C3
Río Curioso (A) 43 H2
Río Damas 34 D6
Río de Cancosa (B) 13 G3
Río de la Colonia 43 F1
Río de la Invernada 31 G4
Río de la Laguna o Salinas (A)
   27 G3
Río de la Sal (A) 25 H2
Río de las Nieves 41 G5
Río de las Taguas (A) 25 G2
Río de la Troya (A) 23 H4
Río del Carmen 25 F3
Río del Cazadero 22 D6
Río de Leiva 27 F5
Río del Jagüe (A) 23 G5
Río del Medio (Ata) 23 E5
Río del Medio (Coq) 25 G3
Río de los Patos (A) 27 H4
Río del Rocín 27 F5
Río del Sobrante 27 E5
Río del Tránsito 22 C6
Río de Montosa 23 E5
Río de Olivares 29 G3
Río Desaguadero (B) 11 H2

Río Diguillín 33 F1
Río Dumo 33 E5
Río Duqueco 33 F3
Río Ecker (A) 41 H6
Río Elqui 25 E4
Río El Volcán 29 H4
Río Fénix Grande (A) 41 H4
Río Figueroa 23 E3
Río Frío (A) 39 G2
Río Frío 21 F1
Río Frío 39 F3
Río Futa 34 C4
Río Futaleufú 39 F2
Río Gallegos (A) 48 B3
Río Grande (A) 31 G3
Río Grande 15 G6
Río Grande 27 F1
Río Grande 53 E3
Río Guatulame 27 E1
Río Guenguel (A) 41 H3
Río Huaqui 32 D3
Río Huasco 22 B6
Río Hueinahue 35 F5
Río Hueyelhue 36 C1
Río Hueyusca 36 C2
Río Huichahue 35 E1
Río Hurtado 25 F6
Río Ibáñez 41 F3
Río Illupel 27 E3
Río Iñaque 34 D4
Río Inio 38 C2
Río Isluga 13 F1
Río Itata 30 B6
Río Itatita 33 E3
Río Japón 52 D3
Río Jorquera 23 E4
Río Juncalito 21 F6
Río la Esperanza 32 C4
Río Laguna Grande 22 D6
Río Laja 32 D2
Río la Potranca (A) 45 H1
Río Larqui 33 E1
Río Lauca (B) 11 G5
Río Lauca 11 E5
Río Lavas (A) 43 H6
Río Licán 35 E6
Río Liguay 30 D5
Río Limarí 24 C6
Río Lincanquén 32 B4
Río Lircay 31 E3
Río Lista (A) 43 H3
Río Llico 36 C2
Río Lliuco 36 C1
Río Lluta 10 B4
Río Loa 14 C2, 14 D4, 15 F2
Río Lollelhue 34 D5
Río Lonquén 30 B6
Río Lontué 31 E2
Río López 36 D2
Río Los Choros 24 D2
Río Los Cipreses 29 F6
Río los Fatillos (A) 27 G1
Río Máfil 34 D4
Río Maipo 28 D4, 29 G5
Río Malleco 33 E5
Río Manantiales (A) 27 G2
Río Manflas 22 D5
Río Mañihuales 39 F6
Río Manrique (A) 27 H2
Río Matancillas (A) 27 G3
Río Mataquito 30 D2
Río Maule 30 D3, 31 F4
Río Maullín 36 D3
Río Mauri (B) 11 G1
Río Mayer (A) 43 G5

Río Medina 38 C1
Río Melado 31 E4
Río Melchor (A) 25 G6
Río Mendoza (A) 29 H1
Río Mercedario (A) 27 G5
Río Minco 33 F4
Río Molina 29 G3
Río Mostazal 27 E1
Río Muco 33 E6
Río Mulchén 33 E4
Río Nahue (A) 33 G2
Río Nef 41 E6
Río Negro (A) 27 G2
Río Negro (A) 29 H6
Río Negro (Lag) 36 D3
Río Negro (Lag) 37 E6
Río Neuquén (A) 33 H2-H3
Río Nevado 23 F4
Río Nilahue 35 E6
Río Ñires (A) 43 H4
Río Ñirihuau (A) 37 H2
Río Ñuble 30 D6
Río O'Higgins 52 D1
Río Oro (A) 43 H1
Río Oro 52 C1
Río Oscar 52 C1
Río Palena 39 G3
Río Pangal 29 G5
Río Pascua 43 F4
Río Peladas (A) 23 H2
Río Pellahuén 32 B6
Río Penitente 47 H4
Río Perquilauquén 31 E6
Río Pichay 34 C4
Río Pichileufú (A) 37 H2
Río Pico (A) 39 H4
Río Picoiquén 32 C4
Río Pillaguasi (A) 23 H4
Río Pillunleufu 35 E5
Río Pilmaiquén 34 D6
Río Pingueral 32 C1
Río Pinotalca 30 B3
Río Polcura 33 F2
Río Primero 25 G3
Río Puelche 31 G4
Río Puelo 37 G4
Río Pulido 23 E4
Río Pulul 33 G6
Río Puntra 36 C4
Río Purapel 30 C4
Río Quiapo 32 B3
Río Quiburcanca 11 E5
Río Quilimarí 26 D5
Río Quillén (A) 35 G3
Río Quillén 32 D6
Río Rahue 37 E1
Río Ramadillas 23 E5
Río Ranquil 33 G5
Río Rapel 25 F6
Río Rarinco 32 D3
Río Reloca 32 C4
Río Relún 32 B5
Río Remehue 35 E4
Río Renaico 32 D4
Río Risopatrón 39 F4
Río Roble (A) 43 H3
Río Romera (A) 33 H6
Río Rucue 33 F3
Río Sajama (B) 11 F5
Río Salado (A) 31 H2
Río Salado (Ant) 15 F5
Río Salado (Ant) 15 G6
Río Salado (Ata) 21 E5
Río Sama (P) 10 A3
Río Samo Alto 25 E5
Río Sanaya (B) 11 G6

Río Sancarrón 25 G3
Río San Juan 52 A2
Río San Martín 53 E2
Río San Pedro 15 G4
Río San Salvador 14 D5
Río Seco (Tar) 10 D4
Río Seco (Coq) 25 G4
Río Simpson 41 G3
Río Tarde (A) 43 H2
Río Teno 31 E1
Río Tirúa 32 B6
Río Tinguiririca 28 D6
Río Tinguiririca 31 G1
Río Toconce 15 G5
Río Todos Santos (B) 11 F6
Río Toltén 34 C2
Río Tordillo (A) 31 G2
Río Traiguén 32 D5
Río Trani 34 D5
Río Trocoman (A) 33 H4
Río Tulahuencito 27 F1
Río Tupungato (A) 29 H2
Río Turbio 23 E3
Río Turbio (A) 37 G5
Río Turco (B) 11 G4
Río Valdivia 34 C4
Río Valle del Cura (A) 25 H3
Río Valle Hermoso (A) 27 G1
Río Varvarco (A) 33 H1
Río Vergara 32 C4
Río Vilama 15 G6
Río Vilcura 33 F5
Río Vodudahue 37 F6
Río Volcán 27 G5
Río Yelcho 39 E1
Río Zamora 45 G5
Río Zapaleri 18 D1
Río Zapato 52 D3
Segunda Angostura 48 C6
Seno Agostini 52 B5
Seno Aisén 41 E2
Seno Almirantazgo 52 C4
Seno Brenton 52 B4
Seno Darwin 52 C6
Seno de las Montañas 47 E3
Seno de Reloncaví 37 F3
Seno Dyneley 51 H4
Seno Dynevo 50 D2
Seno Europa 44 D3
Seno Eyre 44 D1
Seno Franklin 55 F3
Seno Keats 52 A4
Seno Langford 51 E3
Seno Magdalena 52 A4
Seno Otway 47 H6
Seno Owen 52 B4
Seno Penguin 44 D3
Seno Ponsonby 55 E2
Seno Profundo 50 D3
Seno Pulpo 42 C2
Seno Skyring 47 H5
Seno Última Esperanza 47 F2
Seno Unión 47 E4
Seno Ventisquero 39 E5
Ventisquero de la Colonia 40 D5
Ventisquero Grey 45 E6
Ventisquero Jorge Montt 43 E4
Ventisquero Lucía 43 E4
Ventisquero O'Higgins 43 F6
Ventisquero San Quintín 40 D5
Ventisquero San Rafael 40 D5
Ventisquero Steffen 43 E1

RUINS
Ahu Tongariki (EI) 19 G2
Ahu Vinapu (EI) 19 F3

Anakena (EI) 19 G1
Copaquilla 10 D4
El Médano 16 C6
Orongo (EI) 19 F3
Ovahe (EI) 19 G1
San Pedro de Atacama 15 G6

SALT LAKES
Salar Aguas Calientes 21 G1
Salar de Agua Amarga 21 G3
Salar de Aguas Calientes 18 C2
Salar de Aguilar 21 F4
Salar de Arizaro (A) 18 B6
Salar de Ascotán 15 G3
Salar de Atacama 18 A2
Salar de Azufrera 21 G3
Salar de Bellavista 12 C6
Salar de Carcote 15 G2
Salar de Chalviri (B) 15 H6
Salar de Chiguana (B) 15 G1
Salar de Coipasa (B) 13 H2
Salar de Coposa 13 F5
Salar de Empexa (B) 13 F5
Salar de Gorbea 21 G2
Salar de Huasco 13 F4
Salar de Imilac 17 G4
Salar de Incahuasi (A) 18 C5
Salar de Infieles 21 F4
Salar de Jama (B) 18 D2
Salar de Laguani (B) 13 G6
Salar de la Isla 21 G3
Salar de la Laguna (B) 13 G6
Salar de la Laguna Verde (A) 23 G3
Salar de Las Parinas 21 G4
Salar de Llamara 14 C1
Salar del Miraje 14 D5
Salar del Rincón (A) 18 D4
Salar de Maricunga 23 F1
Salar de Navidad 16 D3
Salar de Ollagüe (B) 15 G1
Salar de Pajonales 21 G2
Salar de Pedernales 21 F5
Salar de Piedra Parada 21 G5
Salar de Pintados 12 C5
Salar de Pocitos o Quirón (A) 18 D6
Salar de Pocopoconi (B) 13 G3
Salar de Pujsa 18 C2
Salar de Pular 18 B5
Salar de Río Grande (A) 21 H1
Salar de Seronal 12 C5
Salar de Surire 11 E6
Salar de Talar 18 B4
Salar de Tara 18 D1
Salar de Uyuni (B) 13 H4
Salar Grande (Tar) 12 C6
Salar Grande (Ant) 21 G4
Salar Mar Muerto 17 E3
Salar Punta Negra 17 G6
Salar Quisquiro 18 D2
Salar Sur Viejo 12 D6
Salar Wheelwright 21 G6
Salina de Aguas Calientes (A) 21 H3
Salina de la Laguna Verde (A) 23 G2
Salina de Llullaillaco (A) 17 H6

WATERFALLS
Cascada de los Novios 37 G2
Salto de la Virgen 41 G2
Salto del Indio 35 E6
Salto del Laja 32 D2
Saltos del Petrohué 37 F2

PLANET TALK

Lonely Planet's FREE quarterly newsletter

We love hearing from you and think you'd like to hear from us.

When...is the right time to see reindeer in Finland?
Where...can you hear the best palm-wine music in Ghana?
How...do you get from Asunción to Areguá by steam train?
What...is the best way to see India?

For the answer to these and many other questions read PLANET TALK.

Every issue is packed with up-to-date travel news and advice including:

- a letter from Lonely Planet co-founders Tony and Maureen Wheeler
- go behind the scenes on the road with a Lonely Planet author
- feature article on an important and topical travel issue
- a selection of recent letters from travellers
- details on forthcoming Lonely Planet promotions
- complete list of Lonely Planet products

To join our mailing list contact any Lonely Planet office.

Also available: Lonely Planet T-shirts. 100% heavyweight cotton.

LONELY PLANET ONLINE

Get the latest travel information before you leave or while you're on the road

Whether you've just begun planning your next trip, or you're chasing down specific info on currency regulations or visa requirements, check out the Lonely Planet World Wide Web site for up-to-the-minute travel information.

As well as travel profiles of your favourite destinations (including interactive maps and full-colour photos), you'll find current reports from our army of researchers and other travellers, updates on health and visas, travel advisories, and the ecological and political issues you need to be aware of as you travel.

There's an online travellers' forum (the Thorn Tree) where you can share your experiences of life on the road, meet travel companions and ask other travellers for their recommendations and advice. We also have plenty of links to other Web sites useful to independent travellers.

With tens of thousands of visitors a month, the Lonely Planet Web site is one of the most popular on the Internet and has won a number of awards including GNN's Best of the Net travel award.

http://www.lonelyplanet.com

LONELY PLANET TRAVEL ATLASES

Conventional fold-out maps work just fine when you're planning your trip on the kitchen table, but have you ever tried to use one – or the half-dozen you sometimes need to cover a country – while you're actually on the road? Even if you have the origami skills necessary to unfold the sucker, you know that flimsy bit of paper is not going to last the distance.

"Lonely Planet travel atlases are designed to make it through your journey in one piece – the sturdy book format is based on the assumption that since all travellers want to make it home without punctures, tears or wrinkles, the maps they use should too."

The travel atlases contain detailed, colour maps that are checked on the road by our travel authors to ensure their accuracy. Place name spellings are consistent with our associated guidebooks, so you can use the atlas and the guidebook hand in hand as you travel and find what you are looking for. Unlike conventional maps, each atlas has a comprehensive index, as well as a detailed legend and helpful 'getting around' sections translated into five languages. Sorry, no free steak knives...

Features of this series include:
- full-colour maps, plus colour photos
- maps researched and checked by Lonely Planet authors
- place names correspond with Lonely Planet guidebooks, so there are no confusing spelling differences
- complete index of features and place names
- atlas legend and travelling information presented in five languages: English, French, German, Spanish and Japanese

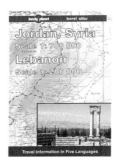

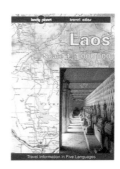

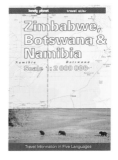

LONELY PLANET GUIDES TO SOUTH AMERICA

Argentina, Uruguay & Paraguay
Discover some of South America's most spectacular natural attractions in Argentina; beautiful handicrafts in Paraguay; and Uruguay's wonderful beaches. This indispensable guide is packed with countless insider tips to help independent travellers make the most of a visit to this diverse area.

Bolivia
From lonely villages in the Andes to ancient ruined cities and the spectacular city of La Paz, Bolivia is a magnificent blend of everything that inspires travellers. This guide is packed with all the practical details a traveller needs.

Brazil
From the mad passion of Carnaval to the Amazon – home of the richest and most diverse ecosystem on earth – Brazil is a country of mythical proportions. This detailed guide will help you enjoy it all.

Brazilian phrasebook
Whether you are looking for the best *onda* or after a *pensão* to rest, this handy phrasebook is packed with useful words and phrases to help travellers make the most of their visit.

Chile & Easter Island
Where will you find arid deserts and alpine peaks, wild rivers and Pacific beaches, tranquil lakes and rugged fiords, volcanoes and lush forests? This guide covers all the adventurous activities and presents hundreds of ways to explore this spectacular country of contrasts.

Colombia
Colombia is the land of the unknown, an independent travellers' frontier, and this comprehensive guide is the essential resource to this country of contrasts.

Ecuador & the Galápagos Islands
Ecuador offers a wide variety of travel experiences, from the high cordilleras to the Amazon plains – and 1000 kilometres west, the fascinating Galápagos Islands. This guide is an essential companion for independent travel to this enchanting country.

Guatemala, Belize & Yucatán
Travellers to Guatemala, Belize and the Yucatán peninsula of Mexico will discover a wealth of spectacular sights. Climb a volcano, explore colourful highland villages or laze your time away on coral islands and Caribbean beaches. The lands of the Maya offer a fascinating journey into the past.

Latin American Spanish phrasebook
From Texas to Patagonia – you'll never be stuck for words. So whether it's a *camión* in Mexico, a *micro* in Chile, or a *chiva* in Colombia, you'll be on the right bus with the help of this book.

Peru
From the floating islands on Lake Titicaca to the ancient Inca city of Machu Picchu, Peru offers the traveller a wealth of spectacular attractions. This nuts-and-bolts guide will tell you how to make the most of your time and money.

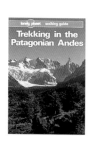

Quechua phrasebook
Quechua is the ancient 'Mouth of the People' of the Inca Empire. It is still widely spoken in parts of Peru and Bolivia, and a little knowledge will enhance your travel.

South America
This comprehensive guidebook travels the length and breadth of the continent, from the Darién Gap to Tierra del Fuego, and includes Easter Island, the Galápagos Islands and the Falklands (Islas Malvinas).

Trekking in the Patagonian Andes
This detailed guide gives complete information on 28 walks, and lists a number of other possibilities extending from the Araucanía and Lake District regions of Argentina and Chile to the remote icy tip of South America in Tierra del Fuego.

Also available:

Full Circle: A South American Journey *by Luis Sepúlveda*
Full Circle describes 'a journey without fixed itinerary' into the heart of South America. Exiled Chilean writer Luis Sepúlveda paints vivid, sometimes surreal pictures of a continent where the distinction between reality and fiction is often blurred.

LONELY PLANET PRODUCTS

AFRICA
Africa on a shoestring • Arabic (Moroccan) phrasebook • Cape Town city guide • Central Africa • East Africa • Egypt • Egypt travel atlas • Ethiopian (Amharic) phrasebook • Kenya • Morocco • North Africa • South Africa, Lesotho & Swaziland • Swahili phrasebook • Trekking in East Africa• West Africa • Zimbabwe, Botswana & Namibia • Zimbabwe, Botswana & Namibia travel atlas

ANTARCTICA
Antarctica

AUSTRALIA & THE PACIFIC
Australia • Australian phrasebook • Bushwalking in Australia • Bushwalking in Papua New Guinea • Fiji • Fijian phrasebook • Islands of Australia's Great Barrier Reef • Melbourne city guide • Micronesia • New Caledonia • New South Wales & the ACT • New Zealand • Northern Territory • Outback Australia • Papua New Guinea • Papua New Guinea phrasebook • Queensland • Rarotonga & the Cook Islands • Samoa • Solomon Islands • South Australia • Sydney city guide • Tahiti & French Polynesia • Tasmania • Tonga • Tramping in New Zealand • Vanuatu • Victoria • Western Australia
Travel Literature: Islands in the Clouds • Sean & David's Long Drive

CENTRAL AMERICA & THE CARIBBEAN
Central America on a shoestring • Costa Rica • Cuba • Eastern Caribbean • Guatemala, Belize & Yucatán: La Ruta Maya • Jamaica

EUROPE
Austria • Baltic States & Kaliningrad • Baltics States phrasebook • Britain • Central Europe on a shoestring • Central Europe phrasebook • Czech & Slovak Republics • Denmark • Dublin city guide • Eastern Europe on a shoestring • Eastern Europe phrasebook • Finland • France • Greece • Greek phrasebook • Hungary • Iceland, Greenland & the Faroe Islands • Ireland • Italy • Mediterranean Europe on a shoestring • Mediterranean Europe phrasebook • Paris city guide • Poland • Prague city guide • Russia, Ukraine & Belarus • Russian phrasebook • Scandinavian & Baltic Europe on a shoestring • Scandinavian Europe phrasebook • Slovenia • St Petersburg city guide • Switzerland • Trekking in Greece • Trekking in Spain • Ukrainian phrasebook • Vienna city guide • Walking in Switzerland • Western Europe on a shoestring • Western Europe phrasebook

INDIAN SUBCONTINENT
Bangladesh • Bengali phrasebook • Delhi city guide • Hindi/Urdu phrasebook • India • India & Bangladesh travel atlas • Indian Himalaya • Karakoram Highway • Nepal • Nepali phrasebook • Pakistan • Sri Lanka • Sri Lanka phrasebook • Trekking in the Indian Himalaya • Trekking in the Nepal Himalaya
Travel Literature: Shopping for Buddhas

ISLANDS OF THE INDIAN OCEAN
Madagascar & Comoros • Maldives & Islands of the East Indian Ocean • Mauritius, Réunion & Seychelles

MIDDLE EAST & CENTRAL ASIA
Arab Gulf States • Arabic (Egyptian) phrasebook • Central Asia • Iran • Israel & the Palestinian Territories • Israel & the Palestinian Territories travel atlas • Jordan & Syria • Jordan, Syria & Lebanon travel atlas • Middle East • Turkey • Turkish phrasebook • Trekking in Turkey • Yemen
Travel Literature: The Gates of Damascus

NORTH AMERICA
Alaska • Backpacking in Alaska • Baja California • California & Nevada • Canada • Hawaii • Honolulu city guide • Los Angeles city guide • Mexico • Miami city guide • New England • New Orleans city guide • Pacific Northwest USA • Rocky Mountain States • San Francisco city guide • Southwest USA • USA phrasebook

NORTH-EAST ASIA
Beijing city guide • Cantonese phrasebook • China • Hong Kong city guide • Hong Kong, Macau & Canton • Japan • Japanese phrasebook • Japanese audio pack • Korea • Korean phrasebook • Mandarin phrasebook • Mongolia • Mongolian phrasebook • North-East Asia on a shoestring • Seoul city guide • Taiwan • Tibet • Tibet phrasebook • Tokyo city guide
Travel Literature: Lost Japan

SOUTH AMERICA
Argentina, Uruguay & Paraguay • Bolivia • Brazil • Brazilian phrasebook • Buenos Aires city guide • Chile & Easter Island • Chile & Easter Island travel atlas • Colombia • Ecuador & the Galápagos Islands • Latin American Spanish phrasebook • Peru • Quechua phrasebook • Rio de Janeiro city guide • South America on a shoestring • Trekking in the Patagonian Andes • Venezuela
Travel Literature: Full Circle: A South American Journey

SOUTH-EAST ASIA
Bali & Lombok • Bangkok city guide • Burmese phrasebook• Cambodia • Ho Chi Minh city guide • Indonesia • Indonesian phrasebook • Indonesian audio pack • Jakarta city guide • Java • Laos • Laos travel atlas • Lao phrasebook • Malaysia, Singapore & Brunei • Myanmar (Burma) • Philippines • Pilipino phrasebook • Singapore city guide • South-East Asia on a shoestring • Thailand • Thailand travel atlas • Thai phrasebook • Thai Hill Tribes phrasebook • Thai audio pack • Vietnam • Vietnamese phrasebook • Vietnam travel atlas

THE LONELY PLANET STORY

Lonely Planet published its first book in 1973 in response to the numerous 'How did you do it?' questions Maureen and Tony Wheeler were asked after driving, bussing, hitching, sailing and railing their way from England to Australia.

Written at a kitchen table and hand collated, trimmed and stapled, *Across Asia on the Cheap* became an instant local bestseller, inspiring thoughts of another book.

Eighteen months in South-East Asia resulted in their second guide, *South-East Asia on a shoestring*, which they put together in a backstreet Chinese hotel in Singapore in 1975. The 'yellow bible', as it quickly became known to backpackers around the world, soon became *the* guide to the region. It has sold well over half a million copies and is now in its 8th edition, still retaining its familiar yellow cover.

Today there are over 180 titles, including travel guides, walking guides, language kits & phrasebooks, travel atlases and travel literature. The company is one of the largest travel publishers in the world. Although Lonely Planet initially specialised in guides to Asia, we now cover most regions of the world, including the Pacific, North America, South America, Africa, the Middle East and Europe.

The emphasis continues to be on travel for independent travellers. Tony and Maureen still travel for several months of each year and play an active part in the writing, updating and quality control of Lonely Planet's guides.

They have been joined by over 70 authors and 170 staff at our offices in Melbourne (Australia), Oakland (USA), London (UK) and Paris (France). Travellers themselves also make a valuable contribution to the guides through the feedback we receive in thousands of letters each year.

The people at Lonely Planet strongly believe that travellers can make a positive contribution to the countries they visit, both through their appreciation of the countries' culture, wildlife and natural features, and through the money they spend. In addition, the company makes a direct contribution to the countries and regions it covers. Since 1986 a percentage of the income from each book has been donated to ventures such as famine relief in Africa; aid projects in India; agricultural projects in Central America; Greenpeace's efforts to halt French nuclear testing in the Pacific; and Amnesty International.

'I hope we send people out with the right attitude about travel. You realise when you travel that there are so many different perspectives about the world, so we hope these books will make people more interested in what they see.'

– Tony Wheeler

LONELY PLANET PUBLICATIONS

AUSTRALIA (HEAD OFFICE)
PO Box 617, Hawthorn 3122, Victoria
tel: (03) 9819 1877   fax: (03) 9819 6459
e-mail: talk2us@lonelyplanet.com.au

UK
10 Barley Mow Passage,
Chiswick, London W4 4PH
tel: (0181) 742 3161   fax: (0181) 742 2772
e-mail: 100413.3551@compuserve.com

USA
Embarcadero West,155 Filbert St, Suite 251,
Oakland, CA 94607
tel: (510) 893 8555   TOLL FREE: 800 275-8555
fax: (510) 893 8563
e-mail: info@lonelyplanet.com

FRANCE
71 bis rue du Cardinal Lemoine, 75005 Paris
tel: 1 44 32 06 20   fax: 1 46 34 72 55
e-mail: 100560.415@compuserve.com

World Wide Web: http://www.lonelyplanet.com/

CHILE & EASTER ISLAND TRAVEL ATLAS

Dear Traveller,

We would appreciate it if you would take the time to write your thoughts on this page and return it to a Lonely Planet office. Only with your help can we continue to make sure this atlas is as accurate and travel-friendly as possible.

Where did you acquire this atlas?

Bookstore ☐ In which section of the store did you find it, i.e. maps or travel guidebooks? ....

Map shop ☐   Direct mail ☐   Other ....

How are you using this travel atlas?

On the road ☐   For home reference ☐   For business reference ☐

Other ....

When travelling with this atlas, did you find any inaccuracies?

....

....

....

How does the atlas fare on the road in terms of ease of use and durability?

....

Are you using the atlas in conjunction with an LP guidebook/s?   Yes ☐   No ☐

Which one/s?..............................

Have you bought any other LP products for your trip?..............................

Do you think the information on the travel atlas maps is presented clearly?   Yes ☐   No ☐

If English is not your main language, do you find the language sections useful?   Yes ☐   No ☐

Please list any features you think should be added to the travel atlas.

....

....

....

Would you consider purchasing another atlas in this series?   Yes ☐   No ☐

Please indicate your age group.

15-25 ☐   26-35 ☐   36-45 ☐   46-55 ☐   56-65 ☐   66+ ☐

Do you have any other general comments you'd like to make?

....

....

....

....

....

P.S. Thank you very much for this information. The best contributions will be rewarded with a free copy of a Lonely Planet book. We give away lots of books, but, unfortunately, not every contributor receives one.